THEATRE LIBRARY ASSOCIATION

The Theatre Library Association is a non-profit organization established in 1937 to advance the interests of all those involved in collecting and preserving performing arts materials and in utilizing those materials for purpose of scholarship. The membership is international and includes public and private institutions, as well as librarians, archivists, curators, conservators, private collectors, historians, teachers, designers, actors, writers and all other interested persons.

The Theatre Library Association meets annually to conduct its business in the fall of each year. It presents a day of conferences and programs during the annual meeting of the American Library Association, and frequently cooperates with other professional and scholarly organizations in the sponsorship of symposia, events and publications.

The Theatre Library Association publishes **Broadside***, a quarterly newsletter,* **Performing Arts Resources***, an annual journal, and occasional conference compendia.*

It is governed by a constitution which provides for a board of directors elected by the membership and officers elected by the board.

THE THEATRE LIBRARY ASSOCIATION BOOK AWARDS

Two awards are presented annually for books of unusual merit and distinction in the fields served by the Association.

The George Freedley Award, *established in 1968, honors work in the field of theatre published in the United States. Only books with subjects related to live performance will be considered. They may be biography, history or criticism.*

The Theatre Library Association Award, *established in 1973, honors a book published in the United States in the field of recorded performance, which includes motion pictures, radio and television.*

Works ineligible for both awards are textbooks; anthologies; collections of essays previously published in other sources; reprints; works on dance, ballet and opera; plays and similar dramatic works. Translations of significant works, other than play texts, will be considered. Entries will be judged on the basis of scholarship, readability and general contribution of knowledge to the fields served by the Association. No galley sheets or proofs will be accepted. Books nominated for awards must be published in the calendar year prior to the presentation of the awards and must be received no later than March 1 of the year following publication.

Nominations are to be submitted in writing to the Chair, Book Awards Committee, in care of the Theatre Library Association, 111 Amsterdam Avenue, New York, N.Y. 10023.

PERFORMING ARTS RESOURCES, the annual publication of the Theatre Library Association, is designed to gather and disseminate scholarly articles dealing with location of resource materials relating to theatre, film, television, radio, video and popular entertainments; descriptions, listings, or evaluations of the contents of such collections, whether public or private; and monographs of previously unpublished original source material.

Please submit query letter only. All manuscripts must be typed cleanly on one side only, double-spaced, and adhering to the style and method described in the MLA Style Sheet, Second Edition. Discs will not be accepted. Please include a list of appropriate illustrative material; black-and-white photographs and line cuts will be used at the discretion of the editor.

Please send all correspondence to:

Performing Arts Resources
c/o B. Cohen-Stratyner
Theatre Library Association
111 Amsterdam Avenue
New York, New York 10023

PERFORMING ARTS RESOURCES

Edited by
Barbara Naomi Cohen-Stratyner

VOLUME SIXTEEN

TAKING THE PLEDGE AND OTHER PUBLIC AMUSEMENTS

Published by the Theatre Library Association

The Library of Congress catalogued this serial as follows:
Performing Arts Resources
    Vols. for 1974 – issues by the Theatre Library Association
    ISSN 0360-3814
1. Performing arts – Library resources – United States – Periodicals
I. Theatre Library Association
Z6935.P46   016.7902'08   75-646287
ISBN   0-032610-13-0

Produced by Sans Serif, Ann Arbor, Michigan.
Manufactured in the United States of America,
This serial is printed on acid-free paper.
A member of the Council of Editors of Learned Journals.

TABLE OF CONTENTS

FROM THE EDITOR

Performing Arts Resources is published annually by the Theatre Library Association to make available reference materials to scholars, curators, and the staffs of performing arts and general-readership libraries. In our past volumes, authors have announced major discoveries, presented new translations and revealed unearthed treasures in all of the performing and broadcast arts.

In Volume Sixteen, the treasures are performance texts from 19th century America. Half of the volume deals with Temperance as subject and motivator of performance. John W. Frick introduces George Cruikshank's serial illustration, *The Bottle*. T. P. Taylor's dramatization of that morality poem is reproduced in full from a British 1850s script followed by the illustrated text of Cruikshank's *The Gin-Shop*. An essay on narrative voices in songs, broadsides and dramas and a bibliography of dialogues, exercises, recitations and dramas on Temperance complete the section.

Four articles on popular entertainment forms using archival material follow. Their subjects – Henry Clay Barnabee and his travelling players, a Battle of Gettysburg Cyclorama, a George M. Cohan vaudeville sketch, and a cadet corp theatre group – show the vast range of performance in 19th century America. The articles by X. Theodore Barber and Eugenia Everett were presented as papers at the International Symposium on Popular Entertainments in 1987.

We invite all readers to submit proposals for articles in upcoming *Performing Arts Resources*. Volume 17 will focus on broadcast media – radio, television and beyond. Volume 18 will consider the roles of archivists, curators, scholars, collectors, and audience members in the development of exhibitions.

"VICTIMS OF THE BOTTLE, FROM PRINTED PAGE TO GILDED STAGE: T. P. TAYLOR'S DRAMATIZATION OF GEORGE CRUIKSHANK'S SERIAL ILLUSTRATIONS, *THE BOTTLE*"

by John W. Frick

Prior to the beginning of the nineteenth century, few Americans would have been tempted to criticize the alcohol consumption of their countrymen since, in the opinion of one European visitor, "everyone drank all of the time." During the seventeenth and eighteenth centuries, the drinking of alcoholic beverages was practically a national pastime open to all citizens regardless of class, race, gender or age. A healthy ration of rum or whiskey routinely accompanied the evening meal in American households, and constituted the obligatory offering to visitors to the home; farmhands in the fields were regularly served liquor on breaks because it was widely believed that alcohol was a stimulus to hard work and was a means of renewing strength after physical exertion; and, drinking played an integral role in American politics, with elections often won or lost depending upon which candidate distributed the most free liquor to voters.

Not only were such "traditional" practices exempt from criticism from the medical community and the clergy, but these influential professions actively championed the consumption of liquor. Doctors routinely touted the medicinal benefits and nutritional value of distilled and fermented beverages, while ministers of all denominations disseminated the view that rum, gin, whiskey and brandy, were "the good creatures of God." Drunkenness, both professions maintained,

JOHN W. FRICK teaches at the University of Virginia at Charlottesville. He is the author of *New York's First Theatrical center: The Rialto at Union Square*.

was to be shunned, but drinking in moderation was to be regarded as a benign and wholesome practice.

While drinking involved all ages and social groups and women were as prone as their husbands to imbibe at home, the social pressures on men to drink were especially intense. While still children, white males were taught to drink by their fathers; ten year old boys at play imitated their fathers' drinking habits; adolescents regarded drinking in a tavern as a symbol of manhood; and grown men became accustomed to the free flow of alcohol in the workplace and at all social events, as well as in the home. Men were further encouraged to drink at all-male events like the militia muster and the local political meeting, or at the quintessential eighteenth-century "males – only" institution, the public house or tavern. At the latter, where convention dictated that every drinker "treat in turn" by periodically buying a round for those assembled, alcohol consumption during an evening frequently exceeded a half-pint of hard liquor per-person and drunkenness was a common occurrence.

By the early 1820s, the problem of intemperance was further exacerbated by an abundance of cheap whiskey. At prices between 25 to 50 cents per gallon, even a poorly paid laborer who received one dollar per day could afford to get drunk several times each week. By 1830 the "average" American consumed over five gallons of whiskey annually and, one-eight of the male population fell into the category of "confirmed drunkards." Given this level of alcohol consumption, it is little wonder that in the early years of the nineteenth century America was characterized by a British traveller as a "nation of drunkards" and a significant segment of the American populace was beginning to feel the need to challenge traditional drinking practices.

The epidemic of intemperance came at a time when American society was in a state of rapid transition from its colonial youth to post-revolutionary adolescence and was experiencing both the growing pains associated with unprecedented expansion and the insecurity and self-doubt which accompanied a transformation from a rural, agricultural society to an urban, industrialized society. Viewed in this context, drinking began to be perceived, not as the "good creature" and social necessity of earlier times, but rather as a serious threat to public order, as destructive of the moral fabric of the country, and as a major impediment to future economic expansion.

As early as 1813, temperance societies, established expressly to combat the spread of drunkenness in American society, asserted that "poverty and misery, crime and infamy, diseases and death, are all the natural and usual consequences of the intemperate use of ardent spirits."[1] Relying upon this and similar statements, reformers were quick to place responsibility for the growing list of social ills squarely upon the shoulders of the drunkard, the tavern owner and the distiller.

In their quest for converts to their cause, temperance advocates portrayed the bottle as the destroyer of the American family and as a competitor for the family paycheck, for if the family breadwinner were to spend the money required for food and lodging on liquor, starvation, eviction and misery would inevitably follow. If, they continued, the husband and father were to return home in a drunken state, wife beating, family desertion, and assaults on children would be the natural consequences. At a time in history when many Americans were convinced that the best hope for the survival of the republic lay in the rising generation, reformers' arguments, which warned that intemperance jeopardized the next generation and virtually guaranteed urban chaos, were especially effective.

In the early years of temperance agitation, reformers also capitalized upon Americans' deep-rooted fear of anything which would deprive them of their independence and individuality. Human beings, temperance literature postulated, were fallible creatures unable to resist strong temptations and, as such, were especially vulnerable to lapses of will power which would lead to intemperance. In this scenario, such intemperance would invariably lead to a dependency upon alcohol which reformers equated with "voluntary slavery." Following, as it did, the United States' second war against an imperialistic and potentially enslaving power, temperance advocates' thesis that liquor deprived those who used it of their free will found a receptive audience.

Early temperance advocates also found a ready and willing source of converts in America's emerging middle-class, to whom self-mastery, and self-discipline were the necessary means to both material and personal success. Faced with fears of a growing urban disorder which threatened their new-found status and norms, and ambitious to remain upwardly mobile, middle-class men and women stressed individual industry and sobriety as necessities in the home, in the social arena, and in the workplace, where the inefficiency and absenteeism caused by drinking cost manufacturers profits and drunkenness increased the likelihood of industrial accidents.

To disseminate their message (or propaganda, as their opponents labeled it), temperance societies and individual reformers adopted a wide variety of forms: novels, journals, pamphlets, short stories, poems, illustrations, broadsides, songs, plays and, later in the century, vaudeville and music hall sketches, panoramas and magic lantern shows. Nowhere, however, was temperance propaganda more immediate, more vivid and more effective than on the stage where the lurid horrors of drunkenness and its consequences could be portrayed with alarming realism. In its ability "to touch the feelings with electric quickness," the temperance melodrama resembled the Washingtonians' "experience" speeches.[2]

While in actual practise the temperance drama exhibited a wide range of variations (*The Drama of the Earth* is patterned upon an epic poem, *The Poisoned Darkys* resembles a minstrel hall sketch, and *The Drunkard's Daughter* is little more than a static dialogue between participants), the vehicle of choice of most temperance playwrights was the conventional nineteenth-century melodrama.[3] With its simple, clearly delineated characters, its polar extremes of morality, its violent emotionalism and exaggerated sensationalism, and its clear resolution with virtue rewarded and evil punished, the melodrama could readily be utilized for "moral suasion" and as a means of urging spectators to sign "the pledge."[4]

Commonly, temperance dramas began with a scene of domestic tranquility and middle-class well-being designed to illustrate what the drunkard-to-be has to lose and to introduce the family he risks sacrificing should he pursue his habit.[5] While the drinker is most frequently a mechanic or artisan, occasionally (*Fifteen Years of a Drunkard's Life; Saved, or A Woman's Influence*) he is socially superior (an aristocrat, a wealthy merchant, or an intellectual), thus increasing the height from which he will fall.[6] Shortly after the audience is shown the family at its happiest, the author invariably introduces the bottle, pairing the temptation (demon rum) with the weak and vulnerable victim-to-be. In the 1840s, with significant public opinion aligned against moderate drinking and widespread belief that teetotalism was the ultimate solution to the nation's social ills, temperance dramatists frequently portrayed the "fatal first glass" as an integral part of the early dramatic action.

Once taken, the first drink set into motion a chain of cause and effect which led rapidly to the helplessness and enslavement of the drinker. Visually, the desperation of the victim's condition was depicted by a deterioration in his physical appearance which became increasingly bloated, pale and disheveled, and in a corresponding decline in the surrounding environment. Consistent with reformers' belief that intemperance opened the path to all other vices, the drunkard was also frequently shown gambling, stealing, cheating, swearing, or embezzling funds from his workplace, all certain signs of a drinker's decline.

If this were the extent of the havoc wrought by a drunkard, the picture would most certainly have been poignant; but, temperance authors, convinced as they were that the ultimate victim of intemperance was the American family, reserved their most emotional moments for the portrayal of the plight of the drunkard's wife and children. Tied irrevocably to the drunkard by both law and cultural norms, women and children were forced to undergo, not only the hardships which the drunkard encountered, but the physical beatings or verbal tirades which were the outward manifestations of his frustrations and guilt. Thus, the innocent family members were likewise victimized and enslaved by alcohol and the drunkard became victimizer as well as social victim.

While the bottle of whiskey or rum was the actual villain of a temperance drama and Temperance the real hero, both were frequently personified by on-stage representatives: Temperance by the confirmed teetotaller or reformed drunkard (Romaine in *Ten Nights in a Bar-room*, Rencelaw in *The Drunkard*); the evils of liquor by the distiller or tavern owner (Tom Lloyd in *Three Years in a Man-trap*; Simon Slade in *Ten Nights in a Bar-room*; Hiram in *Aunt Dinah's Pledge*).[7] The latter, because he took food from the mouths of children to line his own coffers, was regarded as morally bankrupt and, in keeping with the nineteenth-century concept of poetic justice, was marked for madness, violent death, or other suitable punishment by the end of the play.

Left unchecked, the drunkard's disintegration in a temperance melodrama inevitably led, not only to his death and/or madness, but to catastrophic consequences for his family as well. Vernon, the drunkard in *Fifteen Years of a Drunkard's Life* accidently kills his wife before perishing himself; while Reckless in *The Drunkard's Children* murders his wife in a drunken rage and ultimately goes mad, his daughter is driven to commit suicide, and his son is forced into a life of drunkenness and crime and death in a squalid prison cell.[8]

More frequently, however, in a less catastrophic type of temperance melodrama, the drunkard encounters and survives a personal crisis (usually the death of his wife or a child or a premonition of his own death or the death of a loved one), finally realizes the consequences of his actions, repents, signs the temperance pledge and, in the final moments of the drama, is "reconciled to sobriety" and redeemed. The immediate benefits of signing the pledge are further reinforced by picturing the reformed drunkard restored to health, surrounded by his loving family and often materially rewarded by promotion at work or increased public recognition and status.

In creating an unrepentant drunkard and sending an entire family to its destruction, T. P. Taylor's *The Bottle* (1847) is clearly catastrophic in its outcome and strongly resembles darker temperance melodramas like *Fifteen Years of a Drunkard's Life*. Taylor's drama and other plays with the same title, as well as a poem by H. P. Grattan and a swiftly produced serial novel, were all based upon a series of eight drawings (Tableaux I-VIII) by political caricaturist George Cruikshank, who had gained a measure of fame by illustrating the works of Dickens, William Harrison Ainsworth, and others. After a lifetime of excessive drinking and bohemian living, in 1847 Cruikshank abruptly signed the pledge and embraced the cause of total abstinence. In keeping with the zest which he had shown for his previous habit and life in general, Cruikshank joined the temperance lecture circuit and also published two dramatic denunciations of intemperance in the graphic serial mode: *The Bottle* (1847) and *The Drunkard's Children* (1848).

When Cruikshank's *The Bottle* first appeared in September 1847, a writer in *Douglas Jerrold's Weekly Paper* predicted that it "will, no doubt, be speedily placed upon the stage. (It) is a perfect domestic drama, in eight acts."[9] Londoners didn't have long to wait for the fulfillment of this prophesy, for on October 18 Taylor's dramatization opened at the City of London Theatre. As the playbill for the opening declared, this was the "official" version of *The Bottle* with "the whole of the Tableaux under the Personal Superintendance of MR. GEORGE CRUIKSHANK." The official stage adaptation of Cruikshank's drawings was followed by unsanctioned productions at the Royal Pavilion, the Standard, the Britannia Saloon and the Albert Saloon, all within two weeks of the opening of the Taylor/Cruikshank production.

The second of Cruikshank's graphic series, *The Drunkard's Children*, followed a pattern similar to that of *The Bottle*. The official version, written by T. P. Reynoldson and staged at the Surrey Theatre in July of 1848 by Cruikshank himself, was quickly copied, with spinoffs appearing at three other theatres within days of the Surrey opening. One of these, J. B. Johnstone's adaptation, eventually gained as much popularity as the Reynoldson script.

Both *The Bottle* and *The Drunkard's Children* retained a following in London for nearly a decade, but unfortunately, the same was not true in America where *The Drunkard's Children* was never successfully produced and where neither Taylor's version of *The Bottle* nor a rival dramatization by G. D. Pitt achieved much success. The initial opening of *The Bottle* at the Park Theatre on November 15, 1847 was regarded as a "comparative failure;" a second production at the Bowery in December of the same year was similarly received even with C. W. "Drunkard" Clarke in the role of Richard Thornley; and a third attempt at Barnum's American Museum in January of 1849, again starring Clarke, ran for what George Odell termed a "harrowingly long run." Thereafter, *The Bottle* was revived only sporadically and then only as a vehicle for actor benefits. By the early 1850s, all versions of the play had vanished from the New York stage, with only an occasional production staged in the hinterlands.

The relative commercial failure of *The Bottle* not withstanding, it (along with its companion piece, *The Drunkard's Children*) remains as the one of the best examples of the type of temperance melodrama in which the path of intemperance is traced to its inescapable conclusion, the destruction of an entire family, and the plight of the drunkard is portrayed in all of its unrelenting horror.

ENDNOTES

[1] Benjamin Rush cited in Jack S. Blocker, *American Temperance Movements: Cycles of Reform*. (Boston: Twayne Publishers, 1898), p. 7.

[2] Defined by Blocker, the Washingtonian experience speech was a narrative of a reformed drunkard's "personal odyssey from debauchery to sobriety." These speeches, delivered directly to an audience and detailing the story of a drunkard's decline and eventual salvation, resembled temperance melodramas in both structure and emotional appeal.

[3] John Kidder, *The Drama of the Earth* (New York: Adolphus Ranney, 1857); H. Elliot McBride, *The Poisoned Darkeys* (New York: Wehman Bros., 1877); J. E. McConaughy, *The Drunkard's Daughter* in S. Hammond, *A Collection of Temperance Dialogues for Divisions of Sons, Good Templar Lodges and other Temperance Societies* (np, 1869).

[4] While no one thought to keep statistics on the total number of audience members who signed the pledge, figures recorded by Dr. and Mrs. Robinson's temperance troupe are considered representative. In nine years (1843 to 1852) of exhibiting temperance dramas from New Hampshire to San Francisco, they estimated that of the estimated 200,000 spectators, over 10,000 signed the pledge.

[5] In isolated cases like *Little Katy, or the Hot Corn Girl*, the drunkard was a woman, but generally the drunk was male.

[6] Douglas Jerrold, *Fifteen Years of a Drunkard's Life* (New York: Samuel French, Publisher, nd); Edwin Tardy, *Saved, or A Woman's Influence* (Clyde, Ohio: A. D. Ames, Publisher, nd)

[7] William W. Pratt, *Ten Nights in a Bar-room* (New York: Samuel French, Publisher, nd; W. H. Smith, *The Drunkard, or the Fallen Saved* in Richard Moody, *Dramas from the American Theatre, 1762–1909* (Boston: Houghton Mifflin Company, 1969); Charles H. Morton, *Three Years in a Man-trap* (Camden, NJ: New Republic Print, 1873; Harry Seymour, *Aunt Dinah's Pledge* (New York: Wehman Bros, c. 1850)

[8] Jerrold, *Fifteen Years of a Drunkard's Life*; J. B. Johnstone, *The Drunkard's Children* (London: Samuel French, 1848). In the original, "sanctioned" script by Reynoldson the daughter, Emma, succeeds in committing "self-murder." In Johnstone's version of the play, the daughter, here named Mary, jumps from London Bridge, but is saved by the temperance spokesman.

[9] *Douglas Jerrold's Weekly Paper* 11 September 1847, p. 1141 cited in Martin Meisel, *Realizations: Narrative, Pictorial, and Theatrical Arts in Nineteenth-century England* (Princeton: Princeton University Press, 1983), p. 125.

"THE BOTTLE"

A Drama,

IN TWO ACTS,

FOUNDED UPON THE GRAPHIC ILLUSTRATIONS

OF

GEORGE CRUIKSHANK, Esq.

BY

T. P. TAYLOR,

AUTHOR OF

Wildfire Dick, The Seasons, The Waits, The Destruction of the Bastile, &c. &c

THOMAS   HAILES   LACY,

WELLINGTON   STREET,   STRAND
LONDON.

*First Performed at the City of London Theatre,
on Friday, October 1st, 1847.*

The Scenery, entirely new by Mr. ROBERTS, of the T. R. Covent Garden, Mr. ROBERTS, JUNR., Mr. MORELLI, and Assistants. The Music, by Mr. MINGAYE. The Machinery by Mr. CAWDERY, and Assistants. The Properties and Appointments by Mr. PURVIS, and Assistants. The Dresses by Mr. CANTOR, Mr. LEWIS, and Assistants. The Drama and Tableaux under the personal superintendence of Mr. R. HONNER.

𝔓rogramme of Scenery, Characters, &c.

ACT I.

RICHARD THORNLEY (*a Mechanic, an irresolute
Character)* .... MR. LYON.

JOE (*his Son, a boy of 5 years old—a character not
formed)*.. MASTER PEARCE.

GEORGE GRAY (*Associate of Thornley—an Improving
Character)* .... MR. H. T. CRAVEN.

SAM CODDLES (*Pot-boy at the "High-Mettled
Racer"—a Speculative Character)* .... MR. J. HERBERT.

DOGSNOSE (*a Determined and Sporting Character)* . MR. E. B. GASTON.

SERJEANT CRANK (*in the Recruiting Service—a Real
Character to be seen any day between London Bridge,
and Stone's End, Borough)* .... MR. SMITH.

BINKS, No. 242 (*an Official Character)* .... MR. PEARCE.

SPIKE (*a Sworn Broker and Appraiser—a Character too
generally known)* .... MR. ERSSER JONES.

MR. MOREWORTH (*a Master Engineer—a Worthy
Character)* .... MR. MORELLI.

THE HON. GRANGE HOUNSLOW, (*a Roue, and
an every day Character)* .... MR. E. F. MARSHALL.

RUTH THORNLEY (*Wife of Richard—an Exemplary
Character, the Real Friend and Monitress)* .... MRS. R. HONNER.

ESTHER CLARE (*her Friend—an Industrious Character)* .... MRS. E. F. SAVILLE.

EMMA THORNLEY (*Daughter of Richard*) .... Miss Bird.
KITTY CRUMP (*a Shoe Binder — rather an Envious
Character*) .... Mrs. R. Barnett.

An Apartment in the House of Thornley.

TABLEAU THE FIRST.

THE HAPPY HOME. – The Bottle is brought out for the first
time – The Husband induces his Wife to take a Drop.

Finsbury Square — Parlour of the "High-Mettled Racer."

A Street in the Neighborhood of Finsbury.

TABLEAU THE SECOND.

He is discharged from his Employment for Drunkenness – They
Pawn their Clothes to supply the Bottle.

A VIEW NEAR THE BANK.

TABLEAU THE THIRD.

An Execution sweeps off the greater part of their Furniture, and
he seeks for Comfort in the Bottle.

A Lapse of Three Years is supposed to take place between the First
and Second Acts.

ACT II.

RICHARD THORNLEY (*a Depraved Character*) ... Mr. Lyon.
JOE (*his Son — a New Character*) .... Master Dolphin.
GEORGE GRAY (*in the East India Service — a Martial
Character*) .... Mr. H. T. Craven.
DOGSNOSE (*a Determined Character of the Worst
Order*) .... Mr. E. B. Gaston.
SAM CODDLES (*an Amateur Pastry-Cook, and Vendor
of Pies — an Improving Character*) .... Mr. J. Herbert.
BINKS (*a Rising Character*)...................... Mr. Pearce.
SPIKE (*an Auctioneer, Broker, and Appraiser — an Unre-
lenting Character*) .... Mr. Ersser Jones.

RUTH THORNLEY (*a Neglected Character*) .... Mrs. R. Honner.

ESTHER CLARE (*an Amiable Character*) .... Mrs. E.F. Saville.

EMMA THORNLEY (*Daughter of Richard—a Rising Character*) .... Miss Wentworth.

KITTY CRUMP (*an Altered Character*) .... Mrs. R. Barnett.

MRS. WOLF (*a Lodging-House Keeper—an Avaricious Character*) .... Mrs. Griffith.

MRS. GRUMP (*a Feeling Character*) .... Miss Davis.

Exterior of a Public House in the vicinity of Moorfields.

TABLEAU THE FOURTH.

Unable to obtain Employment, they are driven by Poverty into the Streets to beg, and by this means he still supplies the Bottle.

Chick Lane—Apartment of Esther the Needlewoman.

TABLEAU THE FIFTH.

ABODE OF MISERY.—Cold, Misery, and Want, have destroyed their youngest Child—but he still consoles himself with the Bottle.

Moorfields.   Thornley's Room.

TABLEAU THE SIXTH.

Fearful Quarrels and Brutal Violence, are the natural consequences of the frequent use of the Bottle.

A Garret in the Residence of Thornley.

TABLEAU THE SEVENTH.

The Husband, in a furious state of Drunkenness, kills his Wife with the Instrument of all their Mischief.

Room in the House of Mrs. Grump.—An Apartment in Bethlehem.

THE BOTTLE HAS DONE ITS WORK !

It has destroyed the Infant and the Mother—it has brought the Son and Daughter to Vice and the Streets, and left the Father a hopeless Maniac.

For Costumes—*See* Series of Plates.

THE BOTTLE.

ACT I.

SCENE I. – *A neatly-furnished Room in Thornley's House.*

TABLEAU THE FIRST. – "THE HAPPY HOME; THE BOTTLE IS
BROUGHT OUT FOR THE FIRST TIME."

RUTH, THORNLEY, EMMA, and NED discovered.

THORN. Come, wife, one glass—only one, now; just take a glass.

RUTH. You know my aversion, Richard, to drink of any kind; it is the
forerunner of all evil. The very sight of it inspires me with dread; I am very sorry
you have brought it here.

THORN. Now, you're getting low-spirited; I couldn't have done a better
thing. What so good for cheering low spirits as a glass of this? When one's
vexed, now, or put out, this brightens one up, and makes all right again.
Recollect, this day ten years we were married; and I ask you to oblige me, and
you won't. It makes one think you're not so happy as you professed to be.

RUTH. Happy, Richard! let the stranger enter, and judge, from the comfort
around, whether I could be otherwise than happy; let him look at the smiling
faces that grace our humble board, and say whether it speaks not of contentment! No, Richard, I have been very happy; and to oblige you, though unwill-
ingly, I will taste with you, and pray that it may continue, that no dark cloud
may shadow our humble yet happy fireside!

THORN. (*hands the glass; she tastes, and puts it down*) That's well; but the
thoughts of a dark cloud shadowing our fireside—what put that in your head?

RUTH. I only hoped, Richard, it might not. (*turns away*)

THORN. Why, how now? there's a tear glistening in your eye. I say, children,
you hav'n't been vexing her, eh?

RUTH. Oh no; they are ever good and dutiful.

THORN. There's something on your mind, and it's no use concealing it. Come I must and will know it.

RUTH. Then since you bid me speak, hear me, Richard, and without anger. It is *that* which causes me sorrow. (*points to bottle*) Its progress is slow, but sure; it is the pest of the humble home; it is the withering curse of the happy circle; the deadly poison that corrupts and withers, changing the good to bad; it fascinates but to destroy; it charms in its progress, but its end is the grave. What reproach so bitter as the term of drunkard? Mark the result that waits upon its victims; they are spurned by their fellow-men as a pestilence; they dread the day, for they cannot brook the eye of scorn, and long for night, that they may shroud themselves in darkness, and deeply drink to banish recollection. I have seen all this – seen it in that family, once so happy, happy as ourselves, whom the demon Drink has claimed. This it is, Richard, that gives me sorrow. Oh! by the memory of our old loves, fly it, shun it, avoid it!

THORN. Why, Ruth, lass, you beat parson at church; you have made me feel so chilly, and I tremble like the leaves when the wind whistles through them; I must just take another glass, to warm me a bit.

RUTH. No, no, Richard; no more, if you love me; cast it from you as you would a loathsome thing, for there is poison in the touch. Do, Richard, do; or its fascinating influence will teach you to love it better far than Ruth. *She* will be forgotten, and *that* will be your only charm.

THORN. (*rises, and takes bottle*) D–n the bottle; I wish I had never seen it. You make me feel so uncomfortable, that sooner than have any more words about it, I'll throw bottle and all away!

RUTH. Do, Richard, do! and it will make me indeed happy to find that my words have awakened your better reason – that I have not spoken vainly. You hesitate –

THORN. Well, you see, Ruth, they do say it be sinful to waste anything; now, this cost a matter of one-and-tenpence, and – and 'tis very good spirit, and I don't think it be right to throw it away. Suppose, now, you felt sickish like, see how handy it would be to have a drop in the house, or in case a friend calls in.

RUTH. As you will, Richard; but for my sake – for the sake of those around you – do not forget yourself as a man; do not forget those who look up to you for support; nor, by the neglect which it teaches, desolate that hearth, once so joyous and happy. (*they embrace; he puts bottle on table, and sinks in chair*)

Enter GEORGE GRAY, D. *in* F.

GEORGE. Good evening, Mrs. Thornley. Ah! Richard, I'm glad to find you at home.

THORN. (*rises and goes to him*) Hush! not a word. (*aside*)

RUTH. Glad to find Richard at home? where else did you expect to find him? or where else, George, at the close of his day's toil, should a father be found, but in the bosom of his family?

GEORGE. True, but I thought—(*looks uneasily at* RICHARD)

THORN. George, won't you take a drop of anything? we've got it in the house. There, wife, now you see how handy it is. (*fills glass*)

GEORGE. No, no; I wouldn't touch a drop for the world.

THORN. Why, this is the anniversary of our wedding-day; you won't refuse to drink the missus's health, and prosperity to the young ones, eh?

GEORGE. I wish them all the good they wish themselves, and long, long days of unmingled happiness; but I won't drink—I darn't; and I'm sure Mrs. Thornley will not think the less of me for refusing.

RUTH. No, George, I admire you the more.

THORN. Well, then, there'll be no harm in my drinking your health, and wishing us all prosperity. (*drinks*)

RUTH. Again, Richard!

THORN. Well, it was only one glass, and 'twere pity to waste it. Ecad! they may say what they like, but there be nought like a drop of good liquor, after all.

GEORGE. I want to speak with you, Richard; but—

THORN. I understand. Wife! hadn't thee better put the children to bed? it be getting late.

RUTH. I hope, George, you havn't come to take him away?

THORN. No; I ain't going out; George has just dropped in to have a chat, and mayhap he'll stop and spend the evening wi' us, and have a social glass. Come, children, give us a buss.

CHILD. Good night, father!

THORN. Good night! (*shakes hands, &c.*)

RUTH. (*aside*) I wonder what made him turn so pale when he saw George?

Exit, L., *with the* CHILDREN.

THORN. Now, George, what makes you look so solid, eh?

GEORGE. You havn't been to work to-day.

THORN. Hush! hush! don't let her know.

GEORGE. I can't blame you for concealing it from her, for I can well guess what her feelings would be; but this is not the first time, by many, that you have absented yourself. Your conduct has been noticed. I need scarcely ask the reason of this change—it is this (*the bottle*); and, from being one of the most sober and industrious men, you are becoming—

THORN. I know—a drunkard! But don't talk about that, don't; I've had enough of it all the evening: but I do like a glass, and that's the truth on't.

GEORGE. You must conquer the feeling, or it will conquer you.

THORN. D—n they preaching! didn't I tell you I'd have no more on't?

GEORGE. I come to warn you as a friend, Richard, and you must hear me; or you may learn that from others which may prove less pleasing. I have that to say which I wouldn't for the world she should hear—you have to-day again been absent.

THORN. Well, they can stop the day's pay, and there's an end of it.

GEORGE. And how many days, and how often, have they done the same, and with no better effect! To conceal the deficiency from your wife, you have resorted to other means – betting with grooms, jockeys, and so on. Your intoxication has been observed; the blow is impending – avert it – there is yet time; and shun for ever the cause of all your miseries – the public-house.

THORN. Look you, George; I thank you for all you have said, and feel it here. I love my home, and heaven forbid that I should destroy its happiness: I love it so well, that if I thought she knew all this, I think it would drive me mad, for I never could bear her just reproof. You speak of the public-house as the cause of misery to me and others; well, let the employers settle with the humble artizan elsewhere, and not compel him to receive his hard earnings on the Saturday at the public-house, which holds out the temptation, and may end in his corruption.

GEORGE. Summon resolution to your aid; all men have fortitude – exert it. I was gradually creeping into the same error, but the debasement and regret I felt enabled me to conquer the temptation: do you the same.

THORN. Well, I will – I will; but things arn't come to the worst yet, eh?

GEORGE. No; but I heard our employer say that intoxication had spread to so great an extent in the factory, that he should put a stop to it, by discharging those who had given way to this fatal vice.

THORN. But there have been others who are worse than me. There's Dognose, now, and –

GEORGE. 'Twas a warning intended for all – for the sober man to avoid the evil, for the drunkard to reflect. The man you have named is no friend to any one, and at bottom idle and reckless. But your wife returns – think upon what I have said; for I mean it friendly, believe me.

THORN. I know – I know you do; but I arn't too far gone yet, am I? No, no; and I won't be led away, nor go to the house again – I won't. But, George, not a word to *her*; she mustn't know – promise that.

GEORGE. I wouldn't for the world cause her a single pang; it is for this reason I have sought you, and with the best intentions. You may rely upon my keeping my word – you keep yours. Good bye! and let to-morrow find you at your business.

THORN. And every other day, George, please heaven! Good bye! and thank you kindly.

Music. – He shakes hands with GEORGE, *who exits,* D. *in* F.

Phew! how cold his words have made me. My blood seems chilled and frozen, and I ain't done anything particularly wrong neither – not more than other men – not so bad. Oh, yes! Richard, you have; you have deceived her, the wife of your bosom – she who has been all truth, love, and confidence; for you have told her a lie, and now you wonder that you tremble. It is the guilt at your heart,

Richard, upbraiding you for the wrong you have done, which makes you feel like a coward. My discharge threatened–and it may come, and with it poverty, ruin, and disgrace. Poverty to them! Drink!–drink, to give me courage, or she will read in my *face* the secret of my *heart*. One glass only, and the *last*. (*drinks*) So!–how it rouses and cheers one; I feel a new man again. But I won't endure these troubles–no, no! I remember, before I took to *this*, I felt quite different: it has changed me, somehow–made me feel fiercer and more irritable, like; but I'll have no more of it–no, not a drop.

Enter RUTH, L.

RUTH. So, George has gone. Rather a hasty visit. Why, how pale you look! No ill news from the factory, I hope; nothing wrong?

THORN. Why, what should there be wrong? You have always unpleasant thoughts in your head! (*testily*)

RUTH. (*mildly*) Well, I only asked; and, from your manner, I fear there is.

THORN. I tell you, no! What has the factory to do with you? Hold your tongue, will you!

RUTH. Richard, we have been married for ten years, without a harsh word being spoken; I hear them now for the first time–nor will it be the last, if you listen not to me: do, do, for it is not the loving husband that is speaking to me now, but the evil spirit within him. (*weeps*)

THORN. There, don't weep, don't: we'll be comfortable as ever; for you know, wife, there is nothing to make us otherwise.

RUTH. Yes, Richard–this! (*points to bottle*)

THORN. Ah! but you know not what I ha' done since you have been away–I took another glass–

RUTH. Another!

THORN. Ah! but hear what for–I took another glass, and I said, You be very beautiful–there's no denying it be good, you know, and cheering, and so on: but it's my last glass, so good bye, for I'll never touch you again.

RUTH. Dear Richard! (*embraces*) and now all things around grow bright again; for I feel the spell of temptation is broken for ever!

Enter Kitty, D. *in* F.

KITTY. Ah! that's as it should be; I like to see everybody happy. I couldn't help giving you a look in, on my road home. How's all the children?

RUTH. Well, and at rest.

KITTY. Ah! it's a fine thing to go to bed early; I've got a lot of shoes to bind, that'll keep me up half the night. Ah! when we're children, we think it hard to go to bed soon; when we grow up, and want to go to bed, we can't. Mr. Thornley's not looking quite so well. I like to make everybody happy!

THORN. I'm well enough–nothing ails me.

KITTY. That's more than they can say at the baker's. Havn't you heard the news?

RUTH. No—what has happened?

KITTY. Well, I thought you'd like to hear—I like to make everybody happy. Ruff's, the baker's, next to the public-house, where they sell the divinest gl—glass of spirits. (*aside*) I see there's a bottle on the table; they might ask me.

RUTH. Well!

KITTY. Their youngest child's dead—measles, they say—teething, I think. By-the-bye, it was the smallest child; but, however, it's gone, poor dear! bad nursing, I'm told—mother drank. (THORNLEY *starts*; RUTH *looks at him*) They don't ask me. Ah! drinking's a bad thing! I like to make everybody happy.

RUTH. It is, indeed!

KITTY. There's one comfort, drinking don't trouble *me* much.

THORN. Hang her chatter. (*aside*)

KITTY. Of course, you've heard the news about the factory?

RUTH. The factory?

THORN. What? what?

KITTY. Oh! Mr. Innocence! Come, I like your pretending not to know; why, there's a lot of men going to be discharged, for missing a day's work, through intoxication. I like to make everybody happy.

RUTH. That can't affect us; my Richard never lost a day, and has ever been sober and industrious: he is not the inmate of a public-house.

KITTY. Oh! then it wasn't you I saw standing at the bar of the "High-Mettled Racer," the other morning? I like to make everybody happy.

RUTH. My Richard! he would scorn to be seen there—you are mistaken.

THORN. Y—yes—of course. Won't you take a glass!

KITTY. Well, I thought I should get some at last. (*aside*) Since you're so very pressing, I'll just take a wee, very wee drop. (*fills glass and drinks*) I do really think this came from my shop. It's very comforting. Talking of comfort, your fellow-workman George Gray is sticking up to Esther Clare, the young milliner. She works in the next room to us ladies. I suppose we shall hear of a marriage coming off soon; but, as I told her, she is very foolish. Families will come, you know, Mrs. Thornley—short wages—children and bread and butter, all day long. I like to make everybody happy.

Enter DOGNOSE, D. *in* F.

DOG. Good evening, all!

RUTH. Why do I dread the presence of that man?

DOG. I'm glad to find you here. I've been waiting for you. You know that job's to come off to-night.

RUTH. Business to-night! It can't be connected with the factory. You're not going out, Richard?

THORN. No, no; I have no wish.

DOG. (*aside*) But I have, and it's necessary–you've got a chance in the stakes. Come down, and know the worst. We shall meet some prime fellows there. Come!

THORN. No, no, let me stay here; I have promised. You can return, and let me know.

DOG. I can't and won't go without you; recollect that–

THORN. Hush! hush! my wife observes. (*aside*)

DOG. As you are so frightened of her, take care I don't frighten her more. (*aside*)

KITTY. Well, I must say it's not over polite to be whispering in presence of ladies; however, I won't be a tax upon anybody. Talking of taxes, the broker's man says this neighbourhood's terribly behind, both in rent and taxes; and that as to-morrow's quarter-day, some of 'em had better look out. He says they've had warning be letter. I like to make everybody happy.

RUTH. That reminds me!–the letter of yesterday–why did Richard conceal it from me?

DOG. You hear and know. I don't suppose, after that, you'll lose the chance of making some money. That sum would make you square. Think! for the time flies.

KITTY. Well, it don't appear that I'm an object of interest here, so I may as well take my departure. Certain persons might offer if they liked, to see certain persons home; but there's no gallantry in these parts. Good night, Mr. Thornley–good night; glad to see you all so well. Good night, Mr. –

DOG. Oh, good night!

KITTY. Ah! I shall live to see that man discharged, Mrs. T. Between ourselves, I've heard that man drinks awful. I like to make everybody happy. (*goes to* D.) Mercy on me! there's a little girl leaning out of window; she'll fall to a certainty. (*calls*) Mr.–your child's falling out of window. I like to make everybody happy.

Exit, D. *in* F.

DOG. Are you resolved?

THORN. Yes, it must be. (*takes up hat*) Wife, I must go out.

RUTH. At this hour, Richard?

DOG. Why, it's an unexpected matter up at the factory; it will put money in his pocket.

RUTH. Richard, tell me, is it indeed to the factory you're going?

THORN. Yes. Why should you doubt?

RUTH. Enough–I will take your word, for you never yet deceived me.

DOG. Pity you didn't ask that party to stay with your good lady; but however, we sha'n't be long.

RUTH. When may I expect you to return?

DOG. Oh, in an hour. The sooner we go, the sooner we shall be back. Come!

don't look so glum; I know it's unpleasant to leave one's home, and the faces that make it so bright and cheering; but business, you know, Mrs. Thornley, must be looked to. Here, take a glass to keep out the cold.

RUTH. Oh, no! Richard doesn't drink.

DOG. Oh, oh! Well, I do. Here's to you, Mrs. Thornley—better times, and soon. (*drinks*)

THORN. Well, I must drink that.

RUTH. Husband!

THORN. One glass—only one. (*drinks*) Now I'm ripe for business.

RUTH. In an hour—remember!

THORN. In one hour.

Exit, D. *in* F.

RUTH. My mind misgives me—but, no! he would not tell me a falsehood. That letter—let me look for that. (*searches drawer*) 'Tis here! Great Heaven! as I expected, from the landlord—"Half-year's rent, due to-morrow; and, if not paid—" (*drops letter*) Half-year's rent due! It was ever paid punctually as the quarter came. Merciful powers! what horrid thoughts are these that fill my mind? I feared the worst, and it has come. Hope, all flies, for he has deceived me. Oh! brain, brain!

Enter KITTY, D. *in* F.

KITTY. Excuse me, Mrs. Thornley; but your husband—

RUTH. Well!

KITTY. I thought you'd like to know where to find him.

RUTH. And that is—

KITTY. At the public-house. I like to make everybody happy.

RUTH. Oh! the deception thickens. Love has fled for ever—confidence broken, for he has told me a lie. What trust can I have in future promises?—what faith can I place in his love? None, none; for he has told me a lie!

KITTY. Dear me, what could have been the cause?

RUTH. This (*shews bottle*) fiend! Thou hast destroyed us; the tempter has come, and ruin stands upon the threshold. (*sinks down*, KITTY *leans over her; closed in*)

SCENE II.—*Finsbury Square—Evening.*

Enter CODDLES *with tray of beer*, R. 1 E.

CODDLES. What a thing is life! Beer, oh! What's the use of talking about being contented with your situation, if your situation ain't worth nothing. I never was cut out for this line o' life; I'm too haspiring—the field and the fancy's my idea. I don't mean the field of Waterloo, or any of them millingtary romantic places, but the turf and the glorious horse-racing—that's my idea; and when I alludes to a ring, I don't mean that little gold hoop that takes man into execution for life, but the noble art of self-defence. Matrimony's all very well, but it's nothing without the mopusses! I want a hieress—and why not? Sometimes heiresses go off with tall footmen, and why not with a middle-sized pot-boy. But such is life! Pot-boys don't go off so well as they did; the servant-girls looks arter the police now—them areas is the ruin of the force, and the cold meat's their destruction. Well, I've taken the favourite against the field, and if the favourite don't turn up trumps, I shall be very much against the field, indeed! Beer, oh!

Enter BINKS, L.

Well, 242, how do you bring it in?

BINKS. What's that to you?

CODDLES. I'll tell you what it is to me—there's a certain young girl as crosses this square, morning and evening; now I've got a certain eye in that quarter, and as I leave you all the run of the servant gals, which has been the potboy's right from time immemorial, I hopes you won't act ungrateful.

BINKS. What do you mean?

CODDLES. Why, if I catches your eye any more in that direction, the eye of the active and gallant officer, 242, is likely to be put to a little inconvenience. (*squares*)

BINKS. Don't you threaten, my lad, or else I may put you to a little inconvenience. Go on with your beer.

CODDLES. And go on with your beat. I won't bring you out your half-pint when the house is closed, so you can save yourself the trouble of knocking.

BINKS. I've got an eye upon your house; I advise you to look out for licensing day. Mind you're not found out.

CODDLES. And I advise the proprietors of areas to look out for their cooks, and lock their coal-cellars. I take a chalk there, I believe. Go on again.

BINKS. Never mind—we shall see who's right. (*a scream heard*, R.)

CODDLES. There, you're wanted.

BINKS. It ain't on my beat.

Exit, L. 1 E.

CODDLES. The odds 'll be in my favour yet, old feller! I don't much like that eye of his being on our house, for there's a till there that I've looked upon as a sort of loan society; and unless this favourite bisness turns up trumps, I'm afraid I shant be able to return any instalments. But such is life. Beer, oh! I must hope for the best; and as a man that ain't married is a sort of Robinson Crusoe on a desolate island, if a hieress don't turn up, I must be contented with Kitty Crump. That's what I call combining arithmetic with worldly policy. Beer, oh!

Exit, L.

Enter ESTHER, R.

ESTHER. I have at length eluded him. I was compelled to seek refuge in a shop, to avoid him. Why am persecuted thus? for the last week he has followed me. I feared to mention it to George. Heavens! here again!

Going; stopped by HOUNSLOW, *who enters,* R.

HOUNS. So, I have you again, my sweet girl. Why do you avoid me thus?

ESTHER. Your attentions, sir, are unpleasant. My conduct to you must have sufficiently expressed my dislike. I beseech you, leave me.

HOUNS. My dear, I am a gentleman, and therefore—

ESTHER. Your actions are not those of one, or you would allow me to pursue my way unmolested.

HOUNS. Am I so terrible in appearance, that it causes you to behave thus? Let me explain my intentions: you have fascinated me—I love you—I am rich, you (excuse me) are poor.

ESTHER. And for that reason you insult me. You call yourself a gentleman— are your actions like one? Let me pass.

HOUNS. Not yet. Scold as you will, I have (whatever my qualifications may be) sufficient discernment to admire a pretty face, when I see it. As I said before, I am rich—can offer you a carriage, jewels, and—

ESTHER. The name of wife? No, you would make me one of those who, too late repenting, untimely die neglected and forgotten. Go from me, sir; humble and hard as my lot is, I prefer it to all the allurements of the gauds you offer— which dazzle but to betray. (*crosses,* R.)

HOUNS. No, no, we don't part so. I don't think you can refuse me a kiss, at any rate, conscientiously.

ESTHER. I will again cry for help to those who will resent it.

HOUNS. Do so; but it is fortunate that there is no one by to resent it.

Endeavours to kiss her. GEORGE *enters,* R., *turns her suddenly from him, and stands in centre.*

GEORGE. You are mistaken; there is one who will not only do that, but, if necessary, punish.

ESTHER. George!

GEORGE. Don't be alarmed; I shall not suffer my anger to get the better of my reason. Harkye, sir! this young girl is betrothed to me, and though humble in circumstances, has no right to submit to insult; but rather, as a woman, should be protected, even by those who are supposed to set the example to the humble classes as a pattern of conduct, and invariably forget to do it. You rail at our behaviour, but do you ever look upon your own? Oh, no; all that you and such as you do is just and proper; but what the hard-working artisan does, is very bad indeed.

HOUNS. I'm decidedly getting the worst of this. Have you done?

GEORGE. I have—and shall merely content myself by adding, that having now found that she has a protector, you will probably be more guarded in your conduct, not only to her, but to others, lest you receive that punishment which you have deserved, but fortunately escaped.

Exit with ESTHER, L. 1 E.

HOUNS. I've decidedly got the worst of this. I must find out who my young spark is. I will be even with him yet. I have persevered strongly for a whole week, and to no purpose, it appears. Well, the wine I drank at the tavern may have fired my blood, and carried me too far; I must now strive to obliterate the sting of my defeat.

Exit, L. 1 E.

SCENE III.—*Parlour at the "High-Mettled Racer."*

DOGNOSE, RICHARD, TYKE, *and* MEADOWS, *at cards; others looking on.*

DOG. That's mine!

THORN. Ill luck! nothing but ill luck!

DOG. Come, another game! Recollect to-morrow.

THORN. Right. (*clock strikes twelve*) Do you hear that?

DOG. Well, twelve o'clock; what of it?

THORN. What of it? A world to me! We have been here four hours.

DOG. Well!

THORN. I promised to return in an hour.

DOG. What of that?

THORN. I'll tell you what of that. I have done to-night what I never did in my life before—stayed away from my home; I have kept *her* waiting, and watching; listening to every foot-fall, and I can see her disappointment as plainly as if she now stood before me—I can see her watching the hands of the clock, and the minutes, to her drag along so slowly, they seem hours; she gazes upon the light before her—to her, it burns more dimly than ever she has noticed it before; perhaps, for a moment, she feels overcome by sleep, but she wakes up, and suddenly again looks upon the hour; she thinks of rest, but she feels that she cannot sleep—her thoughts are elsewhere—she's thinking of her husband, of the father of her children, and where is he? Oh! where! (*falls in chair*)

DOG. Just ring the bell, will you? Cards is very exciting, and losing puts the nerves out of order.

Enter CODDLES, L. 1 E.

CODDLES. Now then, if there's any further orders, you must give 'em now, or else have 'em at the bar.

DOG. Well, fill these measures again.

CODDLES. Yes, but who's to pay? You know he's parted with his last shilling. Master's lent him a pound–and–

DOG. What are you talking about? Do you think we can't pay?

CODDLES. I see, you are the winners. My eye, if the favourite against the field don't come off the winner, what'll become of me?

THORN. Who's that spoke about the last shilling?

CODDLES. Why, *I* did, merely because there happened to be a recruiting serjeant at the bar, ready for any active young men–nice interesting young men, they look like too–coloured, and very nice work they seem to execute among Turks and other foreigners, if you may believe the engravings. But I'm not to be taken in by your penny plain and twopence coloured; but sitch is life!

Exit, L. 1 E.

DOG. Come, I say, rouse up; another game; think of to-morrow.

THORN. I do, I do; but I think more of her, and of the lie I told.

DOG. Bah! it's only once in the way; if there's a storm, it'll soon blow over. Play again, and see if luck will turn.

THORN. I have nothing left.

DOG. Yes, there's your watch; play, and go in for all you know.

THORN. I know too much.

Enter CODDLES *with beer.*

CODDLES. Now, the beer? (DOGNOSE *about to take it*) But first the money.

DOG. You needn't be so fast–there's my last. (*gives it*)

CODDLES. What a chance for the serjeant!

DOG. Have a drink? (*hands* RICHARD *the pot*) Come, see 'em again; 'tis our last hope, gents; we–we're cleaned out, but will play for this. (*shews watch*)

TYKE. ⎫
MEAD. ⎬ *As you like! (*DOGNOSE *forces* RICHARD *in chair, they play*)
CODDLES. Well, as I'm a bit of a sporting character, I must go in here. I'll take the odds against you.

TYKE. Done!

CODDLES. Half-a-crown to a shilling, and stakes down–very near the last with me; I shall have to go to that till again. (*they play*) Ullo! here's the serjeant turning out of the bar-parlour. Oh! cri', and here's George, the sentimental gent who never calls for anything but half a pint of porter, and never by no means offers to treat you. There's the swell, too–and ain't he been going it with the port wine, neither!

Enter GEORGE GRAY, *followed by* HOUNSLOW *and* SERJEANT CRANK.

HOUNS. That's my man. (*points to* GEORGE)

CRANK. I understand—good figure, and just about the standard measure. Brandy-and-water here, very strong!

CODDLES. Very strong! Oh yes! we always makes it precious strong after twelve; but I suppose as it's for him, it must be pretty decent; strong, I think you said?

Exit, L. 1 E.

GEORGE. (*who has been looking at* RICHARD) Richard, I have been watching you for the last few minutes, and with surprise; you have no business here at this hour; let me entreat you to go home.

DOG. Let him alone; he must finish the game.

GEORGE. Again, I say, he has no right to be here.

DOG. Neither have you.

GEORGE. Nor should I have been, had I not learnt where he was; it was the wish to serve him, as well as those about him, which induced me to come here.

DOG. You're very virtuous, I dare say. He's quite satisfied with the company he's in, ain't you, Richard?

THORN. Of course I am; he wouldn't drink with me this evening and you can't call that man your friend who won't drink with you.

DOG. Oh! no, of course not. This hand will decide it.

Enter CODDLES *with brandy-and-water*, L.

CODDLES. The brandy-and-water.

GEORGE. Lost, unhappy man!

HOUNS. I beg your pardon; we had some words together this night. I had been drinking rather freely, and when the wine's in—you know the rest. I admire your conduct, on behalf of your friend. I say, sup with us, merely to drown all animosity.

CRANK. A fine fellow like you ought to be in the army; active young men, now, are sure to make considerable fortunes. I should say, for you, a serjeant in two months, a lieutenant in four, captain in twelve.

CODDLES. Or a dead man in one. Such is life.

CRANK. Come, drink; you'll not refuse an old soldier—one who has had the honour of being on the field of Waterloo, and serving her Majesty upon many other memorable occasions?

GEORGE. Well, I bear no malice; I will not refuse to drink.

CRANK. Stop! a loyal toast: "Confusion to our enemies, and may the hour never arrive when they can rise up against us!" (GEORGE *drinks*)

CODDLES. And here's "Success to all pot-boys;" and if the hour grows much later, he'll not be able to rise at all.

THORN. Lost! (*throws down cards*) All gone! I am a beggar! Fool! Villain!

GEORGE. All reasoning now with the past is useless; let me entreat you to go home.

THORN. Home! the drunkard has no home. I—I havn't now a shilling in the world, nor a friend to give me one; you can't (*to* DOGNOSE), you won't (*to* GEORGE); and those who gathered round me in my prosperity won't know me now.

GEORGE. Had I the means, I would convince you to the contrary; but to-morrow—

HOUNS. Now's your time—fortunate chanee. (*to* CRANK)

CRANK. (*advances*) What! it never shall be said that a man in my company wanted a shilling; take it, in the Queen's name. (*presses it into his hand*) I love the youth of Great Britain too well to insult them, heaven bless them!

GEORGE. (*offering it to* THORNLEY) Take it, Richard.

THORN. No, I won't; let me go. I have lost all; show me the way to that place which was once a home of joy, which now I have made wretched; let me go, or I shall do somebody a mischief; for my heart's on fire, and my brain—Let me go!

Staggers off, L. 1 E.

GEORGE. I will go with you. He is incapable of assisting himself.

CRANK. Stop! Where shall I find you in the morning?

GEORGE. Why?

CRANK. Because you are the Queen's man—you are enlisted.

GEORGE. I?

CRANK. Didn't you take the money? Your mistress now is Glory.

HOUNS. I saw him give the money, which you accepted.

GEORGE. Villain! this is your work; detain me at your peril. (*rushes at* HOUNSLOW—CRANK *seizes him—business and closed in*)

SCENE IV.—*Street.*

Enter SPIKE, L. 1 E.

SPIKE. Up and stirring with the lark; this is as it should be. Here! Tom Ex.

Enter TOM, L. 1 E.

Now, Tom, you keep your eye continually upon No. 9, and go in with the milk—that is to say, when they open the door, which they're safe to do, to take in the milk, you immediately introduce yourself—you understand.

TOM. Yes, sir.

SPIKE. You ought to have been in 13, long ago.

TOM. Yes, sir, but No. 13's artful; they look out o' the winder, and won't open the door.

SPIKE. Did you try a postman's knock at a late hour?

TOM. Yes, and was hanser'd through the keyhole.

SPIKE. Well, what came of the keyhole?

TOM. Why, they said if I had a letter, I must put it under the door.

SPIKE. It's the most artful village I ever had dealings with; they get into debt, and defy the law. Why, there's one man had the impudence to tell me he had received summonses enough to paper a room, and intended to do it. You must get up an accident at 13, watch the husband out, then tell them he's run over, or fell from a ladder. We must get possession.

TOM. Then I'll try No. 9 first.

SPIKE. We shall astonish the neighbourhood to-day—four possessions and one seizure, How about No. 8, next street?

TOM. No. 8 died last night.

SPIKE. Well, he might have settled his accounts first, and expired with honesty and propriety. What did he die of?

TOM. Why, his wife said the thought of an execution upon his goods broke his heart.

SPIKE. Pooh! an execution is just the sort of thing to make a man lively, and exert himself. And, la! how they do cry. I shouldn't be surprised to hear, some day, of a large family getting up such an extensive flood of tears as to drown the broker. The fact is, poor people are a d—d nuisance. Let me see—8, 13, 14—four possessions—one seizure. How about 6, next street?

TOM. No. 6, in the next street, disappeared in the middle of the night.

SPIKE. And cheated us of the levy? Very well! mind, when we make the next levy, we'll make up for the losses. There goes the milk. (*looks off*, R.) Now, away with you; secure No. 9, and I shall be happy.

Exit Tom, R.

I'll astonish the neighbourhood to-day. Let me see. (*looks at memorandum book*)

Enter DOGNOSE, L.

DOG. Broad daylight, eh? A nice night's work we've made of it. I've come off pretty tidy, but I've had hard work for it. Well, a silver watch is worth having.

SPIKE. Hollo! No. 14, is that you?

DOG. What of that?

SPIKE. Death 'll be busy among your ranks; the sworn broker's amongst you. Why don't you act like a gentleman, and let me put the man in? see how he's been waiting about in the cold; you should have compassion. But I don't think, after all, 14, that you're such a bad man as you've been represented. Can't we come to some little arrangement about that silver watch? The brokers are open to all, influenced by none.

DOG. May be.

SPIKE. Now, let me have it; let it go off the rent, and appear in the eyes of your neighbours with all that magnanimity which paying your way inspires. Give me the watch, and keep open your street-door like a free man; turn virtuous, and die a respected father.

DOG. I can't, because I don't happen to be one.

SPIKE. But you have the watch.

DOG. And intend to keep it.

SPIKE. You'll come to be hanged; a man that don't pay his rent can never expect to prosper. No. 14, just wait till I get in possession; I don't wish to make myself unpleasant.

DOG. But when you meet with anything unpleasant, do as *I* do.

SPIKE. What's that?

DOG. Avoid it.

Exit, L. 1 E.

SPIKE. He'll decidedly come to be hanged. Only let me get my executions settled, and then I can go home to breakfast comfortably.

Exit, R.

SCENE V.—*The same as Scene I.*

.TABLEAU THE SECOND.—"HE IS DISCHARGED
FOR DRUNKENNESS."

RUTH, CHILD *with bottle*, RICHARD *in chair*.

RUTH. Ellen (*giving frock*), this dress you will take to—(Oh! that it should come to this!)—to that shop; they will lend you money upon it. There's not a shilling in the house, and you, my poor children, must not go without your breakfast.

ELLEN. And the bottle, mother, which father bade me take—

THORN. Must be filled! it must; if you raise money for one thing, you can for the other.

RUTH. Go, child, go; it's useless to reprove or argue, now—go, child; and you take your sister into the other room.

Exit ELLEN, D. *in* F. BOY *takes* SISTER *off*, L.—RUTH *falls in chair, and sobs.*

THORN. Ruth, is that you again? what are you crying for?

RUTH. Richard, how are we to live?

THORN. Live! why the same as we always did.

RUTH. I cannot reason with you, for reason has fled it's seat, and nothing but corrupt and hideous matters now find place in your bewildered brain.

THORN. What is the time?

RUTH. The hour is considerably past. (*bitterly*)

THORN. Well, at any rate I have returned—

RUTH. To find your situation lost, your wife and family penniless.

THORN. 'Tis false!

RUTH. It is too true; all who were not there when the bell rang were discharged; one or two passed by this door, and mentioned your name, derisively, as one who would suffer with them. And, oh! how, all the live-long night, have I alternately prayed and watched your coming, and as it faded away, and the first blush of morning beamed through the shutters, its faint and sickly light made me sadder still; yet I watched on, until it became broad day. What then met my gaze? not the husband of former days, but one so degraded, that I almost blush to look upon him.

THORN. Well, well, let it pass; there's annoyance enough. Where's the bottle? that's pleasant, and, in trouble, one's only friend. (*sinks to sleep*)

RUTH. Alas! alas! where shall we find friends now? (*sobs*)

Enter ESTHER, D. *in* F.

ESTHER. Ruth, dearest Ruth, I know scarcely how to address you, but—

RUTH. Hush, speak lower; he is asleep, and sleep may prove beneficial.

ESTHER. I wanted to speak to him, for George, who was last night in his company, has not yet returned; they were seen together at the public-house.

RUTH. Another!

ESTHER. How wild you gaze, Ruth? what has happened?—no quarrel, I hope? No, that couldn't be, for he was ever a good man, and a kind father.

RUTH. Esther, the drunkard can never be either. You are yet young; if George was there last night, shun him now, as you would a pestilence. When once the fatal love of drink seizes upon the mind, all that is good and pure fades beneath the one absorbing passion, as the chill and sudden frost will blight the early flower; avoid him, or your home will be made desolate as mine.

ESTHER. Your home?

RUTH. Yes, look there. (*points to* RICHARD) Bad advisers have helped this, but who will aid us now with friendly counsel? Again, I warn you of George Gray.

THORN. (*rising*) Who wants to know about George Gray? I can tell you; he—he has enlisted.

ESTHER. Enlisted!—impossible!

THORN. Oh, no, it's true enough, and serjeant wouldn't let him go, neither. Come wife, come; I'm getting all right again—let's have no more quarrelling; I'll go and make it all right at the factory, and then we'll be as happy as ever.

RUTH. No, Richard, our future happiness depends upon your renouncing—

Enter ELLEN, *with bottle* D. *in* F.

THORN. The bottle! well, I'll only take a glass now and then; but I want one now, to cheer me up.

Enter Tom, D. *in* F., *with warrant*.

What may you want, pray?

TOM. This paper will explain.

RUTH. (*snatches it*) What is this?

TOM. An execution for rent.

THORN. Who has done this?

RUTH. This—the bottle!

SCENE VI.—*A Front Street*.

Enter Kitty *and* CODDLES, R.

KITTY. Here's nice goings on; one would fancy we were living near the Old Bailey, the executions are so busy. Well, certainly I am surprised at the Thornleys'; upright, straightforward people as they seemed to be; but there's no telling anybody now-a-day's, is there, Coddles? You don't seem to be particularly lively—I like to make people happy.

CODDLES. No—such is life! Kitty, there has been a sort of an affection sprung up between us. Have you invested money anywhere?

KITTY. Well, I think that's a question which ought to come from me. What's he aiming at? I like to make everybody happy. I haven't.

CODDLES. Thankye, you've quietly murdered me.

KITTY. What, after I've expressed an affection for you, do you dare tell me that I have quietly murdered you?

CODDLES. That's all right enough; we've all affections—some one way, some another; before I saw you, I had placed my affections upon a *till*.

KITTY. And who was she?

CODDLES. It ain't a she at all—it's a sort of what-to-avoid kind 'o thing, but I couldn't; whenever I've had a go at the *field*, I've always *tilled* it, and it's likely to prove very *harrowing* to my feelings.

KITTY. What do you mean?

CODDLES. Embrace me!

KITTY. Do what?

CODDLES. Embrace me, being positively the last appearance of Mr. Coddles in that character.

KITTY. I can't understand you.

CODDLES. Well, say nothing to Binks; stick to your shoe-binding, and prosper. Finsbury, you've lost your pot-boy.

KITTY. But where are you going?

CODDLES. I don't know. I always did the friendly thing with the half-quarterns; and when you're indulging in that liquid, perhaps you'll think of Coddles. Binks the officer is handy.

KITTY. Ah! you're a weak-minded man.

CODDLES. Well, I may be *weak*, and for that reason I leave you to the *force*.

Exit, L. 1 E.

KITTY. Well, anything in the shape of a man is better than none at all; but for the present, Kitty, your visions of matrimony are all knocked on the head. Never mind, if I can't be happy myself, I'll go and enjoy myself with the miseries of others. I have not lost much in Mr. Coddles, for he had nothing–take nothing from nothing, and nothing remains. Binks has a pound a week, and that consoling.

Exit, R. 1 E.

SCENE VII.–*Same as Scene I.*

TABLEAU THE THIRD.–"AN EXECUTION SWEEPS OFF THE GREATER PART OF THEIR FURNITURE."

SPIKE, TOM, MAN, THORNLEY, *sipping from glass*; RUTH, CHILDREN.

RUTH. Take this away, girl; already it's intoxicating influence stupifies; another glass will sink the man to a level with the brute. (*gives bottle to* ELLEN, *who takes it back*)

SPIKE. (*reading*) Let's see! chest of drawers, eight-day clock, table, mattrass, bed, bedstead, small ditto–

RUTH. You will, perhaps, for the poor children's sake, leave me the little bedstead, will you not?

SPIKE. Nonsense! there's nothing obliging in law; this is the way mothers spoil their children–too much indulgence; let 'em sleep on the floor–make 'em hardy. (*reads*) Large family bible, tea caddy–no real plate, I think–no, only delph–hearth rug, and picture of the village church. Umph! not a Claude or a Reubens–no rising artist–juvenile effort–sell for a shilling.

RUTH. I must beg of you not to take that; it is the picture of the village church where I worshipped as a girl, that saw me wedded in my womanhood; there are a thousand dear recollections connected with it, humble though they be. There was a meadow close by, over whose green turf I have often wandered, and spent many happy hours, when a laughing, merry child; and dearer far it is to me, for beneath a rude mound in that sad resting-place, poor father and mother lie. You won't refuse me the picture?

SPIKE. Well, it ain't worth much, certainly; but you women are such rum'uns, you are. You wouldn't believe it, but one woman begged and prayed for a set of fire-irons, and because I wouldn't let her have 'em, positively fainted. Such funny fancies! One–let's see–I think we've got all–yes–nice healthy seizure this, no rows—not too many tears. This is what I like—it makes things go off so pleassnt. Is the cart ready?

TOM. All right, sir.

SPIKE. Now, we'll go to No. 13.

THORN. Stop! you don't go yet; I heard my wife ask for a small trifle, which you didn't choose to give her; now, I've a fancy for that myself, and I'll see thee d—d before you lay a finger on it. (*snatches picture from* SPIKE)

SPIKE. (*retreating*) Ullo! here, I say, young feller, let's have peace and quietness—no d—d nonsense. Come, let's have it back.

THORN. Touch it, and I'll brain you. (*Raises picture to strike him*)

PICTURE AND END OF ACT 1.

ACT II.

A LAPSE OF THREE YEARS TAKES PLACE.

SCENE I.—*A Street. Public-house,* L. *adjoining a churchyard.*

TABLEAU THE FOURTH.—"HE STILL SUPPLIES THE BOTTLE."

RUTH. And is it thus you employ the means of benevolence? Richard, reflect.

THORN. Reflect! I can't—I daren't; there is no comfort left me now in my sorrow, but this. (*putting bottle in pocket*)

RUTH. Oh! heaven, that ever my children should come to this; I thought to have seen them clinging around our hearth, when age had peacefully stolen upon us, and that they, thriving in the world, would serve to brighten it; but all now has faded—the prospect once so joyous has grown dim and dark, and we may read our fate in the once green leaves that now fall seared and yellow from the tree.

THORN. Ah! you always look on the wrong side of things—always did. I offer you that which would cheer you—It always drives away the blues—but I can't persuade you. Oh! no. you might be happy, but you won't.

RUTH. Happy! look there. (*points to* CHILDREN) Go back to the days when industry brought content, and every face in our humble dwelling wore a smile, for love and esteem were deeply implanted in the hearts of its inmates; and so years rolled on, and then came, like the mildew on the corn, the fatal drink. Slowly but surely was its progress: The man from whose lips a cross word had never fallen, grew angry and excited—the children, whose caresses ever met with smiles, received harsh treatment, and at length blows, and the broken-hearted wife neglect. So, steeped in poverty, the home became a wreck, and the streets at length their refuge. Happy! look at the boy who clung to your knee, the girl who fondled you, the mother who reared them—and read an answer in their rags.

THORN. (*soothingly*) Now, what have I done?

RUTH. (*pointing*) Look.

THORN. I can't stand this, and I won't; if we are in trouble, things may mend, and you should strive to think so. Instead of trying to console one, you try by every means to add to our miseries; but I have a friend here, who defies all the ill-usage in the world, that's one comfort.

RUTH. For a time, Richard, it may; but the day will come when the charm will be destroyed. Its career is marked by sickness and death—early death. The fevered lip and the pallid cheek already proclaim its influence; and, oh! when the fatal hour arrives, what will become of me, and these poor wretched children? If your heart be not deadened to remorse, think, oh! think of them—helpless, friendless, alone!

THORN. Well, I have thought. The girl, she's comely, and can go into service; and as for the boy, why my old pal, Dognose, he's bringing him up to a profitable business.

RUTH. Service for her?—she is too young for servitude, Richard; but for the boy, I must learn the nature of the employment he has to offer: coming from such hands as his, it can be of little good, and I will not have him made the companion of a dishonest man.

THORN. Go on—crush every effort I make to better our condition, do. What is it to you, so that he earns money?

RUTH. Nothing, so that it be earned honestly.

THORN. And why should you doubt?

RUTH. Have I not cause to doubt the actions of a man who first led you by his pernicious counsels to this fell misery. Look at his companions! who are they?—men shunned and avoided. Richard, as yet we are unstained by guilt; add but that, and our ruin is complete.

THORN. You talk of others; what are we? Can we mix with the fine-dressed, or your honest people? You rail at this life, and check every effort to improve it; but my mind's made up, and nothing you can say will alter it.

ELLEN. ⎫
JOE.   ⎬ *Father! mother! we are hungry.*

RUTH. Yes, yes, you have some money.

THORN. No, I have none; 'tis spent—gone—

RUTH. Great heaven! and that which the hand of charity bestowed, has gone to the accursed monster Drink! Oh! but for my children, would I were laid in the cold, still grave. (*weeps*)

THORN. Harkye—if they want food, let them beg for it.

RUTH. Richard, with that word you have withered every hope—all, all is fled, and your only love is there. Oh, heaven! what will become of us? (*leans against house for support*)

Enter SPIKE, R. 1 E.

ELLEN and JOE. Charity, charity! we are hungry.

THORN. Yes—for one who has seen better days.

SPIKE. Charity, pooh! Go and apply at the workhouse—and break stones—and think how comfortable you'll feel when you reflect how many rich and great people—ay! even nobility—are constantly passing over the efforts of your industry.

THORN. That voice! oh, it's you is it? I thought that we had met before. I know you.

SPIKE. Know me! I've no acquaintance in your style, I assure you; and don't know me too much, or else perhaps you will have to know a policeman!

THORN. Of course; to gaol with the beggar; spurn him, crush him, avoid him as you would a reptile—anything to get rid of him. Some years since you wouldn't have so spoken—you wouldn't have dared.

SPIKE. You must have been a very different kind of man, then.

THORN. I was, indeed; but don't rake up the past—it lays too heavy on the brain—don't, it might madden. Well, one false step brought misery to me and mine; that misery you completed, for you swept away all, and left me bare walls. That was the deepest blow, and I never got over it. I thought and thought, and grew sick at heart, and fancy was busy with me, and I drank to drown care, and the spirit of industry fled from me. Well, I am Richard Thornley.

SPIKE. Bless me! dear, dear! the fine moral man of former days, and the virtuous father become—

THORN. What you see—now not ashamed to ask charity of the passer-by. Come, you knew me once; help me for the memory of old days.

RUTH. If not—for—for my children's sake!

SPIKE. I don't know how it is, but poor people will have children; that, to me, is one of the mysteries of London. But, I say, these sports and pastimes of the people of England, this begging business, is dangerous. The police have strict injunctions, and the Mendicity are all alive, oh!

RUTH. Oh, think if a like calamity crept into your happy home, and made it desolate—what would be your feelings? Think of this helpless little one, whose wasted arms enfold me—starving and cold—think, and pity.

SPIKE. I do believe that women were expressly invented for the annoyance of men of business, and brokers in particular; as for children, they're the scarlet-runners of human life, and they spring up as fast. You don't contract any rent now, I hope? (THORNLEY *sighs*) No, of course not. Prudent, too—nothing like honesty—die rather than deceive a landlord, or annoy a broker; the streets and magnanimity—hospitality and the workhouse. (*feeling in his pockets*) There! I've dodged up a little fourpenny for you! Take it, expend it prudently, and while you have it you'll never want money.

Exit SPIKE, L.

THORN. Little enough, but it will answer the purpose. (*going*)

RUTH. Whither are you going?

THORN. To drown care—to kill that which I feel gnawing at my heart—to drive that from me which fires my brain, and makes it beat so madly. I go to fill the bottle.

RUTH. The children, Richard, the children.

THORN. I care not—the bottle must be filled. (*music—throws her from him, and rushes into the public-house*)

RUTH. Heaven, help me! Heaven, help me! (*leans for support against doorway*)

Enter KITTY, R. 1 E.

Joe and ELLEN. Mother! mother! (*crowding round her*)

KITTY. Ruth, Ruth; come, what ails you? Rouse up, as a good woman; I've such good news for you!

RUTH. I am afraid all good news for me will come too late. I have borne much, but 'tis over now, and I feel my heart is broken.

KITTY. Oh, nonsense! I've heard of a party in the next street who wants assistance, and can give you some needlework; look, here's the address. (*gives card*) Now, go to her to-day; you don't know what it may lead to.

RUTH. You are very kind, but I have scarcely any spirits to undertake it; I feel now so forlorn and dejected, that every effort to restore me to myself seems vain.

KITTY. Yes, but you must rally, for your children's sake.

RUTH. For them—oh! yes you are right, for their sakes I will, I must. Deadened as every feeling is now within me, I must not forget that I am a mother, and that it is a sacred duty to protect them to the last.

KITTY. And your husband, he—

RUTH. (*sighs and points*) There!

KITTY. The wretch! oh! these husbands! Well, if I had a man, I should like to have a gingerbread one, 'cause I could first play with, and then eat him afterwards. Oh! if, foolishly entertaining the thoughts of "persons about to marry," the pound a-week was to serve me so—oh! his face and eyes! I like to make everybody happy. But come, come, no more tears; do as I wish, and all may go well. You may again have the little joint on Sundays, and the comfortable family pudding.

RUTH. Well, well, I'll try; it is for this poor thing, and these helpless ones, that I shall pray to heaven to support me in my task. No drudgery, however menial, I would not cheerfully undertake for them, and them alone, for it would soothe my last bitter moments, to know and feel that I had done my duty to them as a mother.

KITTY. The recommending of this needlework, has given me such a stitch, that–Oh! I like to make everybody happy. (*cries*)

RUTH. Don't give way to regret on my account; your words have inspired me with hope, and I feel better now, and stronger than I have done many a day.

KITTY. That's well; I do like to make everybody happy: and let us hope, too, that your husband may reform.

RUTH. Girl, a confirmed drunkard never reforms.

KITTY. Ah! well, well, perhaps it would be better to leave him where he is. Come, leave this place. 'Tis a very cold and biting day; you all seem chilly, and I'll take you to a place where they sell the most delightful–(RUTH *shudders*) Well, well, I forgot; however, I'll walk with you; there's no pride in me: I like to make everybody happy. Come along. (*going*)

Enter DOGNOSE, *very shabby*, R. 1 E.

DOG. So, the very party I've been in search of! I thought I should light upon you somewhere. Ned, I want you.

RUTH. Want the boy? (*clinging to him*)

DOG. Yes, I've got a move a-foot, that'll change all our fortunes; we'll soon set aside those rags. This it is to have a brain.

RUTH. But how? how?

DOG. You'll excuse me, but I know women too well to trust 'em; this is a little private affair, that can't interest any but those concerned. It's a rare good thing, so let that satisfy you.

RUTH. It does not; and if it be so good, and you really mean to serve us, why conceal its nature?

DOG. That's our affair altogether. Where's Dick?

RUTH. Again I ask, what want you with the boy?

DOG. And again I say, I can't tell. Where's thee father, boy?

JOE. There. (*points to public-house*)

DOG. Of course–I need not ask. Here, Dick, Dick!

Exit into house.

KITTY. Come, its' no use stopping here; let them go and sot together; you look after yourself–you'll get no good out of them.

RUTH. No, but I must know about him. What can he want? he is a bad man, and has ever held my husband in his toils, and I cannot go until I have learned.

Re-enter DOGNOSE, *followed by* THORNLEY, *greatly intoxicated*, L. U. E.

DOG. You see, I point out a clear way of making money, and who can object to it? You don't–no; for you see yourself once again settled, and the little bits of sticks about you, and then once more you can hold the world but as the world, and so defy it.

THORN. Of course, of course; do as you like. I know you wish to serve us all.

DOG. There, it's all settled. Don't be under any alarm; I'm going to take him in hand a little while; I've got a sort of errand-boy's place for him, where he'll soon be well fed and clothed.

RUTH. Where is this place? I claim a mother's right to know, and I must and will, before I part with him. (*holds him*)

DOG. Will you be fed, or will you linger up and down the streets cold and starving?

JOE. No, I've had enough of that—I'll go with you. (*runs from* RUTH *to* DOGNOSE)

DOG. Come, boy—a fortune, and speedy.

RUTH. You shall not take him from me—you shall not—I'll die first.

THORN. Die, then.

Music — Throws her off, she screams and falls. RICHARD *staggers against the shop.* DOGNOSE, *with a laugh, darts off with the* BOY.

Scene II. — *A Street.*

Enter CODDLES, *with a penny-pie stall,* L. 1 E.

CODDLES. Here ye are—penny pies, all hot! veal, kidney, or fruit, fine juicy confectionery, all hot! No bidders! such is life. Talk of the romances of real life, here you have it in Coddles; Coddles, who has gone through a great deal, and is likely to go through a great deal more. Everything's going to the dogs, and they do say that a good many of them animals comes to me, but that's imperance; the real somnamberlists, the cats, is set down as going the same journey likewise, which is neither moral nor proper. I think I shall retire from the meat line, and stick to the fruit: then they cannot make any remark—but I shouldn't care so much, if I could only sell them. It's innovation that's ruined this business—the free trade, the unlimited baked potatoe, and everlasting ham sandwich! And what's been the ruin of me? Coddles, reflect:—betting, I believe, morally—*till*, I consider, properly; beer, I think, generally. As the beer has been to the betting, so as the till been to the pot-boy's destruction. Well, the betting business is as strong as ever, and that induced me to take to the pie line. I do a little on the quiet with the boys, in the juicy meat and fancy confectionery. Well, when things come to the worst, they say, they generally mend; as for mending, I'm mended all over. (*shows dress torn*) Ah! well, such is life. Now to look how my book stands. (*takes one out*) 'Ta'n't exactly a betting-book, but a sort of inweigler of the youthful branches. I do a little in the credit line. They say trust not in woman; that's true, if there's a policeman in the case, or anything milingtary; but

I say, trust not in boys, for I think they take a delight in doing the pieman. (*looking over book*)

Enter GEORGE GRAY, *dressed as a corporal*, R. 1 E.

GEORGE. How familiar all around is to me, and how many happy thoughts have been awakened as I passed by each well-known spot? But as yet I have seen no well-loved faces, met no old friends—for strangers dwell where I was ever a welcome guest. I thought, too, the old factory looked more black and grim than ever, and I saw none of my old industrious associates. To be sure, I have been some years away; many may have passed to their last home. Then I thought of her—what can have become of her? I have gone through a great deal, and what may not she have suffered! I must obtain some information, for I cannot bear this suspense. Perhaps this man—Ullo! pieman.

CODDLES. That's me. All hot, all hot—veal or kidney—juicy meat and fancy confectionery. All hot, all hot!

GEORGE. Do you live about here?

CODDLES. Why, I can't say I *live*, but I go about here.

GEORGE. I want to ask you one or two questions, which you probably can answer. How goes on the factory?

CODDLES. Why, it don't go on at all; it's gone off—not like my pies, they always remain on hand. Take a kidney—

GEORGE. What do you mean?

CODDLES. Why, the old man's done—what I intend to do directly—retired from business.

GEORGE. And the factory men?

CODDLES. Oh, they're all scattered here and there; some are getting up in the world, and some poor fellows are down. (*points*)

GEORGE. You remember, then, Thornley and Johnson?

CODDLES. Thornley! Oh, don't I?—don't everybody! If the pieman were as well known and remembered as he, what a flourishing trade he would drive. They call him the publicans' friend, and he supports them so much, that he now needs support himself.

GEORGE. I feared this. Beggary, eh?

CODDLES. Beggary—rags. Ah! out of the whole lot at that factory, there were very few who turned out good for much. There was one exception—George Gray.

GEORGE. Ah! You knew him?

CODDLES. Knew him? I believe you; I was potboy and waiter at the "High-mettled Racer," the very night he was hocussed.

GEORGE. What?

CODDLES. Yes, hocussed; and through a little bit of spite, and for a little bit of money, they managed to get him enlisted.

GEORGE. You are a villain! (*seizes him*)

CODDLES. No, I'm a pieman. Hallo! what's this for?

GEORGE. I'll tell you: I am that George Gray, who has been banished, by foul means, for many a long year, from my home–from those I loved. You assisted in this foul act: dare you–can you look me in the face?

CODDLES. Yes, because I had no hand in it; it was a mix-up between that swell and the serjeant, one of the proprietors of those highly-coloured engravings where a gentleman on horseback, quite pleasant and smiling, is killing every one about him, like one o'clock. It was their doing, not mine.

GEORGE. If I could believe you–

CODDLES. That's what I want–not only you, but everybody; they won't believe in my pies. You can do me a service–try one, and if you meet anybody, recommend–"one trial is all we ask."

GEORGE. Well, be it as it may, let it pass: I am anxious only about the present. Tell me, there was a girl–one Esther Clare–I would know something of her.

CODDLES. Try a mutton. (*offers pie;* GEORGE *turns from him*) No! Well, as for her, she cried a good deal when you went away; I think there was a little simmering of love, like my pies in the oven, when the heat moves the upper-crust, eh?

GEORGE. Go on, go on.

CODDLES. Well, since then–

GEORGE. Yes–(*eagerly*) since then–

CODDLES. She has struggled on, and held life and soul together, by working hard and fast at the needle. It's a very small instrument, that, but it's astonishing how fine and gay it makes folks. I have often thought whether any of these grand people have an idea how many long, long hours are consumed, and how many sleepless nights have been passed and spent, about the finery they wear. Oh, no! they've got it, and they never bestow a thought upon the maker. I am out very late, and when I have returned from my last round, I've seen the light in her window; and her shadow there, working away, night after night, and at an hour when everybody who had a bed had gone to it; and then I have said (that is, if I had sold all the pies): "Heaven bless you!–industry must thrive." But if I hadn't sold all the pies–

GEORGE. Well, if you hadn't–yes, yes–

CODDLES. Why, then, I used to say, "It's d–d hard; here am I, there is she; her fingers work, so do my legs:" and then I have thought, what a pity candles wasn't sentimental, or else they'd say something.

GEORGE. You–you can direct me–

CODDLES. Direct you–I'll shew yon–

GEORGE. Do, do; go and get yourself something to drink, and then–(*offers money*)

CODDLES. Queen's man, eh? Oh! you don't do the pieman that way.

GEORGE. I don't want to enlist you.

CODDLES. Oh, then, give me the money, if you like, but not for drink. I've been in the business once, and I'm afraid. Many and many a good fellow I've seen drop off, through that same drink. First they'd come only once a-day, then two or three times at last whole days; and then came the crying wives, the ragged children, and the man who used to go neat and tidy got shabbier and shabbier; and although (turning a deaf ear to the prayers of wife and children) he has been turned into the streets, the next morning he has turned in again with the opening of the doors: all at once he has been missed—gone to some other house, perhaps? he has, his last—found dead in the streets. I have seen many an honest, industrious chap, clever at his business, led away like this. Drink's the beginning, and the undertaker is the finish; so I reflected, and said, if I must spend money, I'll do it another way. I daren't enter a public-house; the sight of a till would—La! bless me, I—well, I'll show you the way. Money, if you like, but no drink.

GEORGE. Here, (*gives money*) now, quick, for I'm all anxiety.

CODDLES. (*taking it*) A whole half-crown! Pies, perhaps, won't be out to-morrow; Pies will probably see what's to be done in the betting way, and a shilling sweep is likely to come off, and a six-penny Gravesend, probable.

GEORGE. This way, did you say?

CODDLES. First to your left. How a man feels when he has money in his pocket! You won't try a mutton, will you? because to-morrow the juicy confectionery establishment will be closed. Last serenade;—Pies all hot!—this way.

Exit GEORGE, *followed by* CODDLES, L. 1 E.

SCENE III.—*A neat but plain Apartment. The Picture of the Village Churchyard, as in Act I. Scene I., hanging up.*

ESTHER *discovered sewing.*

ESTHER. This is weary work, hardly earned, badly paid, and wearily goes the time, when there are none by to solace, to console. Poor George! I often think of him, and wonder if he ever bestows a thought upon her he once professed to love. Well, if he has forgotten me, I hope he may be happy. If he selects another, he will never get one to love him more fondly or truly than I did—never. (*pausing in her work*) But I must hasten on with my work. Weeks and weeks I have scarcely had any, and now it comes all at once—more than I can get through, and am now compelled to send for assistance. Work, work, work, and yet of no avail; it will not clear away the poverty by which I am surrounded. The dreadful threat of the few things I have got together being taken from me, the fear of being thrust forth homeless, checks every zealous intention, defies all industrious efforts. Well, well, I must try—still struggle on, still struggle on. (*she continues her work—a low gentle tap at the door*) The landlady, perhaps? I must go and quiet her.

Exit, R.

D. *in* F. *opens. Enter* RUTH *timidly.*

RUTH. I beg pardon, but I believe – no one here? This is the direction – yes. (*looking at card*) I hope they will not be long, for I left my poor child, sickly and ill. I fear – great powers! (*looking round the room*) what is here? (*sees picture*) That picture! Years have passed away since I gazed upon it, and the old, old scenes of joy and happiness come back to me. Again I am wandering over the green turf – again I meet the companions of early days – again I see the old village church – the days that are past spring up again in all their brightness: but I do not meet *him* who led me there! no – no – no! Why does it hang there, as if to remind me of the past – to tell me what I might have been? Why, why – (*staggers to chair and weeps*)

Re-enter ESTHER, R.

ESTHER. For the present I have quieted her. (RUTH *sobs*) What's this? A female here, and ill! (*hastens to her*)

RUTH. I beg pardon, but I came to seek for work. I – (*endeavouring to rise, falls back into chair*) Oh!

ESTHER. You are very ill. (*assisting her*) That face! surely I know it; let me look once again. It cannot be! and yet the likeness – Ruth!

RUTH. (*starts up*) Who is it mentioned that name? It seems to conjure up all the bright and happy hours that are past, that never, never will return. (*wildly*) But I beg your pardon – I – I came to ask for work.

ESTHER. Ruth!

RUTH. Again! I have heard that voice before; I was sure of it. I know it now; let me look upon you – say, have we not met before?

ESTHER. Yes, in far happier days. I knew you when your home was joyful. Many years have passed since we have met, but I little thought, when I asked for assistance, that I should meet with you. Ah! Ruth, you are much changed.

RUTH. I know – I know all that you would say; I had a home once. You know what that home was. For myself I care nothing, but I have children; and when I saw that picture, my heart warmed again, and seemed to whisper – hope. You spoke of happier days – they are past.

ESTHER. Dear, dear Ruth, do not speak thus; you know not how glad I am to find that we meet once again. I never dreamt of seeing you again.

RUTH. Nor I, girl; I never dreamt that the storm of adversity would fall so dark and heavily upon me; but it has come, it has. But that picture?

ESTHER. I bought it at a sale. I knew that it had once been yours, and the recollection of the hours, the bright ones we have passed together, induced me to become its purchaser; I bought it for your sake. Oh! Ruth, you know not how it glads me to be enabled to render you assistance. Here is some work I can offer you. Heavens! how pale you look.

RUTH. Yes, I am ill, very ill, and the support which I require will not be needed long; and then poor, poor children, what will become of you?

ESTHER. Think for the best–take it.

RUTH. Bless you! bless you! (*takes it up*)

Enter SPIKE, D. *in* F.

SPIKE. Stop, stop; I beg your pardon, but this moving things off the premises ain't exactly what the law likes.

ESTHER. What mean you?

SPIKE. Why, there's a little trifle of rent in arrear, and every article becomes of value on such occasions, and if we do a little bit of seizure, it seems we shan't have much to carry.

Enter MRS. WOLFE, R.

MRS. W. Now, Mr. Spike, how do you find things?

SPIKE. Good morning, ma'am; things ain't quite so friendly as I could wish. When one sees little articles upon the go, I always think it's time for the broker to–Umph!–you understand.

ESTHER. If you allude to the trifle which I am indebted to you, I am in possession of plenty of work, and in the course of a week–

MRS. W. Course of a fiddlestick! Money, marm, money; that's what I want–that's what I will have.

SPIKE. Shall I put the man in?

MRS. W. Yes; and you put those things down. (*crosses* L. *to* ESTHER) Nice acquaintances you bring to genteel lodging-houses; but you don't take that parcel with you, for all that.

ESTHER. Speak as you will, she shall have it; she has endured bitter misery, almost starvation; she is an old, an early, but a valued friend, and she shall not suffer longer, if I can prevent it.

MRS. W. I can stand a good deal, but I can't stand this–insulted under my own roof–I've come to something, however! this is the beginning and the end–can you pay?

ESTHER. I have already told you. Do as you please, harsh and cruel as are your proceedings will be, I fear not but that the same Providence who has so long watched over me will not desert me now.

RUTH. And all this is through me. Misery, misery, wherever I go; it has fallen heavily upon me. Why, oh! why should I be doomed to bring it to others?

Mrs. W. I don't want no tears, because that performance won't bring the money.

SPIKE. Of course not; they always have the waterworks ready in these cases. I'll just step across the street, and put a man in.

Enter KITTY, D. *in* F.

KITTY. Oh, Ruth! Ruth! I'm so glad I have found you.

RUTH. You are agitated–pale; speak, speak!

KITTY. You're wanted at home immediately; I cannot, I dare not tell you what for. I have been searching for you for two hours; but, go, go–lose not a moment, or you may be too late.

RUTH. Too late! those words imply–It is death.

KITTY. No, no; let's hope for the best–go, go.

RUTH. I see, I know; it is death. Oh! would to heaven it had come here!

Rushes out, D. *in* F.

KITTY. And, now, pray what brings you here?

SPIKE. What, me? Oh, as for me, I'm going to put a man in.

Enter GEORGE GRAY, D. *in* F.

GEORGE. No, you are not; it is more likely that I'm going to put one out. What is your demand?

MRS. W. Three pounds ten–a quarter's rent; and considering the accomodations, very cheap, too.

GEORGE. I will pay it.

ALL. You?

SPIKE. I wish I have put the man in.

ESTHER. This kindness from a stranger!

GEORGE. Stranger no longer. Have a few years so changed me, that you do not recognise me. Esther, have you forgotten me?

ESTHER. Can it be? What! George Gray?

GEORGE. The same George Gray, that ever said he loved you truly, and has now returned to prove it. (*embrace*)

KITTY. Hurrah! And now, Mr. Spike, you may as well take yourself off the premises; instead of a man coming in, there's one to go out.

MRS. W. Lor' bless me! Well, I do like to see people affectionate. Poor thing! well, I always pitied her.

GEORGE. She, thank heaven, will not longer have need of pity; she has one who will protect her for the future, and shield her from all harm. Go, and learn this lesson–Do as you would be done by! go, and repent.

He leads off ESTHER; KITTY *follows*, L., *grinning.*

SPIKE. I say, Mrs. Wolfe, I shall look to you for my fees, because, thinking to get a broker out without his fees, is all d–d nonsense.

Exit D. *in* F. MRS. WOLFE, R.

SCENE IV.—*A wretched Room.*

TABLEAU THE FIFTH.—"THE DEAD CHILD."

THORN. Why do you take the glass from me?

RUTH. Look around. (*points to coffin*) There is my answer.

THORN. I know; but this is a time that one requires something. Taste a drop, Ruth.

RUTH. Why offer me that which has been our bane and curse? It has done its work well; it has brought death at last. Would it had come to me!

THORN. I must have some—I will; my dark thoughts are upon me again. If it was not for this, I'm sure I should go mad. I must, I will have it! (*drinks—a knocking*) Who's there?

Enter DOGNOSE, D. *in* F.

DOG. It's only me. I'm sorry to see this trouble, but what must be, must. Better times will come.

RUTH. To us—never!

DOG. Oh, yes, they will. Look here. (*shows money*)

THORN. Ah! where got you that?

DOG. Oh, never mind where it came from; the sight of it does one's heart good, don't it. I say, haven't I kept my word?

THORN. You have, you have.

DOG. And the beauty of it is, there's plenty more of it from the same shop. I don't think your good lady will look quite so harshly upon me as she did, eh?

THORN. No, no; and to come at such a time too, when we are penniless! Look up, Ruth. Children—yourself—all without food. He—he has brought assistance. Let the boy go and get something. You won't object to this being filled, just as if it were to drink success to better times? (*draws out the bottle*)

RUTH. (*rising*) No, he shall not go; nor with my sanction shall this accursed poison ever enter here more. It has crushed and blighted every hope on earth, and now it bears grim death in its progress. The children need food; I will go for their sakes, but I will not move one step for that. (*points to bottle*)

DOG. Well, well, just as you like; of the two, I'd rather that you would go. Here's a five-shilling-piece; now, get what you like. (*gives it*)

RUTH. Promise me one thing, that on my return I shall find you both here.

DOG. Oh! I'm not going to take him away.

RUTH. There is another promise I would exact; but no, alas! it is too late.

Exit with GIRL, D. *in* F.

DOG. That's well done, if she can only manage to change it; I think she will, for it is a prime counterfeit. I say, Joe, lad, how, do you like the new game, and the new friends I have introduced you to, eh?

JOE. Oh, well! very well!

DOG. To be sure, and I've taken a fancy to you; I've brought you a new jacket, new trousers, and a pair of boots. Take this, and try your luck with it. (JOE *crosses*, R.)

THORN. Stop, stop! I've been thinking, and I don't exactly like—

DOG. Nonsense, there are no other means; besides, the bottle must be filled.

THORN. Right, right! and, over a glass, we'll talk about it.

Exit JOE, R.

DOG. You see, out of evil comes good; you never thought my brain would turn to such advantage, eh?

THORN. No, no; but it would have been better if you had never thought of this.

DOG. Bah! there's nothing to fear; and it's better to risk everything than starve.

THORN. I don't know that; I've got some strange fancies about me, and it seems as if I heard a warning voice.

DOG. Pooh! where should a warning voice come from, I should like to know.

THORN. From there. (*points to coffin*) Something seems to say, Repent, ere it be too late! That word rings in my ears, and seems to grow louder and louder every minute—now! now! Oh! there is something in this.

DOG. The something in this is, that you want the drink. The boy is slow; a few minutes, and—(*a hum of* VOICES *is heard*) What's that? eh! D—n it, the boy is pursued! It's all up, then, if he makes for here. No, he avoids it. Good lad! The mob follow—the police, too; will they take him? A woman hastens to his rescue, it is—(*A cry of* "Stop thief!" *is heard*)

THORN. What cry is that?

DOG. Nothing, nothing; sit still.

THORN. If it be nothing, why do you turn so pale?

DOG. Another moment, and they will have him.

THORN. Him! who? Stand from the door. What's this? The boy is running. (*a cry of* "Stop thief!")
Ha! I see it all! Wretch, you have destroyed him!

DOG. You mustn't interfere, or you will ruin all.

THORN. I will not see him dragged to gaol as a thief, if I can prevent it; lost, degraded as I am, I have still some portion of the father left within me. Stand from the door!

DOG. You shan't pass. (*throws him from him*)

THORN. Oh! for the strength of former days. I am enfeebled, helpless. The warning voice has not spoken in vain; but, oh! may my bitter curse—

DOG. It is too late; if you must curse, let it be upon the cause of all your miseries—the bottle.

RICHARD *sinks into chair. Closed in.*

SCENE V.—*A front Street.*

Enter CODDLES *and* KITTY, R. 1 E.

CODDLES. Oh! don't talk to me; go to your policeman. He'll be on his beat presently. It's no use 'sinivating with me. There's Gravesend and shrimps in the distance, for me—oysters, perhaps—a policeman for you.

KITTY. Don't you talk too fast, or else I shall really be compelled to comply with the anxious urgings of that active officer; but you have been the means of bringing two loving hearts together, and you don't go to the public-house so much, and I like you for that; and I am glad to see that you have taken to a new line of business.

CODDLES. Yes, but you have never bought any of the pies, and I do not like you for that.

KITTY. Then, you know, I always had a partiality for you.

CODDLES. Yes, and you show it by smiling at me, and walking arm-in-arm with the policeman.

KITTY. Well, that was only done because I like to make everybody happy. An old aunt of mine died lately.

CODDLES. Not the old lady with the private property?

KITTY. The very same; and I've been thinking, Sam, that a single life is very lonely.

CODDLES. Yes, and cold of nights.

KITTY. Marriage with loving hearts is pretty—a nice little business, now.

CODDLES. Yes, pastry, for instance—juicy confectionery.

KITTY. I can fancy myself behind the counter.

CODDLES. And my hand in the till. D—n those counters!

KITTY. A thriving business.

CODDLES. Yes, and thriving children; but since you've started the race, I want to know who is come in the winner?

KITTY. Why, upon the promise of amendment, you.

CODDLES. Me! the sole proprietor of the little property, the penny pieman is lost to the inhabitants for ever. Boys, your half-penny friend is gone, never to return.

KITTY. Come, we'll talk it over as we go along.

CODDLES. You may, under existing circumstances, take my arm. (*going*, R.) Stop a bit; if it's all the same to you, we'll go down the next street.

KITTY. Why?

CODDLES. Because I notice a little bit of blue with white buttons crossing the square.

KITTY. Again jealous of the policeman?

CODDLES. No; but it's as well never to give a chance away.

Exit, L.

SCENE VI. – *The Room as before.*

TABLEAU THE SIXTH – "THE QUARREL."

JOE. You shan't hurt my mother.

THORN. What! would you rise up against me? Recollect, I am your father.

JOE. Ah, ah! a pretty father you've been. Look at me, and see what you've done for me.

MRS. GRUMP. Come, I say, good people, don't quarrel: waking one out of one's first sleep, it's shameful. You've had warning to go, and the sooner you do so the better.

Exit, D. *in* F.

THORN. This is all your doing–all. You've ever the bitter word upon your lip, ever taunting; I can't stand it, even from you, and I won't.

RUTH. To-night, you have struck me a blow; years back you would have abhorred yourself for such an act–an act you would not then have dared to contemplate, but the career of misery is closing–thank heaven it is.

THORN. Be silent–there is dreadful feeling upon me–I am not the man of years back, and, as you say, I am changed. Knowing it, beware of me.

RUTH. If it prove my last words, I must speak them: you have brought a deadly curse upon me and mine. But, oh! I pray, beseech you, ere it be too late, repent; for the day will come when you need consolation–no friendly hand to grasp, and you will die regretting and alone.

THORN. I won't hear another word; be silent, or–

Enter DOGNOSE, *hastily*, D. *in* F.

DOG. It's all up–away! They have got scent of the boy–of her–and have traced them to this house.

THORN. What do you mean?

DOG. The bad money; you all will suffer–in plain words, she has betrayed us.

RUTH. How could I do otherwise? I wanted bread for them, when the fraud was detected. I was innocent; what could I do but tell the truth?

DOG. And by so doing you have convicted your boy; his future home will be a gaol.

RUTH. No, no—not him—they will listen—will pity. 'Tis you, and you only are guilty; and 'tis you that shall be given up to justice.

DOG. They are entering the house.

RUTH. You shall not go. If the innocent are to suffer, so shall you. Help! help! (*struggling*)

DOG. Take your hands off. Will you see this?

THORN. No—'tis not he has brought this ruin; your busy tongue has done all. Let him go.

NELL. Father! father!

(*as he is frantically dragging her from him,* DOGNOSE *rushes out,* RICHARD *seizes bottle from mantle-piece. Closed in.*)

SCENE VII.—*Another Room in the Garret.*

Enter DOGNOSE, L. 1 E.

DOG. Perhaps in some of these rooms I may conceal myself till all is over, for I'm well known in my trade, and I have quite enough upon me to convict me. These women, they spoil everything; however, let but this storm blow over, and I get clean away, I shall take the liberty of carrying on my performance in quite another part of the town. (*going*)

Enter CODDLES, R. *He seizes him.*

CODDLES. No, you don't; I happen to have overheard all that you have said. How about that bad shilling eh? You had eleven-pence ha'penny and a juicy hot pie for a bad shilling!

DOG. Let me go, or I'll do you a mischief.

CODDLES. You can't do more than you have done; and as for hurting, cut away—I can stand it. Here, Mr. Binks!

Enter BINKS R.

For the first time you are really wanted. There's the lot, and a very bad lot it is, too.

DOG. It's all up; but I ain't done nothing. Come, Coddles, confess this is all a lark.

CODDLES. Oh, is it? I hope you may find it so. You can try and persuade them to it at the Old Bailey; eh, Mr. Binks?

BINKS. Two bad pieces of money were passed to-night; they have been traced to him.

CODDLES. Ah! then your two bad pieces have made a hit. He may be the author of a hundred pieces.

BINKS. Come, this way. (*dragging him off*)

(*a violent scream is heard, and a cry of* "Murder")

DOG. What's that?
BOTH. A cry of murder!
DOG. By George, he has killed her!
BINKS. Take care of him.

Runs off, L.

CODDLES. You tremble, and look pale. So you know all about this, too. I don't envy you your feelings. Come along. Queer originally, I believe; bad generally, admitted; transportation, certainly, without a doubt. Come along. Ah! would you! I can do it for you.

Drags him off, struggling, R.

SCENE VIII. – *The Room, as before.*

TABLEAU THE SEVENTH – "THE BOTTLE
HAS DONE ITS WORK."

RICHARD *is seized.*

THORN. Ruth! Ruth! What, don't you answer?
BINKS. She will never speak again.
THORN. Never! What's here, then? Why these people? I've done nothing. What does it all mean?
BINKS. Death – by this! (*pointing to bottle*)
THORN. (*involuntarily shrinks, passes his hand wildly across his forehead, and with a mad laugh*) Ha! ha! (The bottle has done its work! (*falls*)

SCENE IX. – *A Room.*

Enter GEORGE *and* ESTHER, R. 1 E.

GEORGE. Don't droop, Esther! Tears are unavailing now, and what is past cannot be recalled.
ESTHER. I thought we should have rendered them so happy – talked of old times, of the days when their hearts were light, and the sun of prosperity shone around them. She was one of my earliest friends, too, and so anxious ever for our welfare; and this to occur after our long, long parting! Oh, George! the return which brought joy to my heart is now deeply shadowed, and I cannot check these tears; for 'tis very hard to lose an old, old friend. And how deep the regret, when by sudden and violent means. Oh, George! do not think me unkind; but indeed I can't help it.
GEORGE. A deep and moral lesson may be learned from this, and I thank heaven that I avoided the pernicious instrument which, years back, tempted me.

ESTHER. But the unhappy husband – is there no hope?

GEORGE. Alas! no. I tremble when I think of his state! His brain's turned – his senses fled – he is unconscious of everything around; his last refuge is the madhouse. Oh! Esther, this – this is too painful to dwell upon; let us leave this place.

ESTHER. Yet I would see her once again – for the last, last time; only to press her hand – to drop a tear in memory of old, old times.

GEORGE. I guess your meaning; it is impossible now to comply with your wish. Come, Esther, you must strive to forget; you must.

ESTHER. Poor Ruth!

GEORGE *sorrowfully leads her out*, R.

Scene X. and Last.

TABLEAU THE EIGHTH – "The Madhouse."

THORNLEY *chained. The* BOY *and the* GIRL, *and the* KEEPER *looking through door.*

JOE. Don't you know me, father?

THORN. Know! what is there to know? Yes; it's warmer here, and better than the cold and muddy streets. I can't tell what has brought this change about, I can't; I've been puzzling my brain, but to no purpose. It don't beat now as it used to do. It's very strange why she don't come; I never knew her quit my side till now. Why don't she come?

JOE. She never will come again. Don't you know? – think!

THORN. I tell you that I don't know; and what have I got to think about? Who are you that ask it?

JOE. Your son.

THORN. What, my son! No, no; he is ragged, and in the streets. My son; he's not such a fine gentleman as you, and yet – say it again.

JOE. Your son.

THORN. There is a mist before me, and I cannot distinguish your face; but the voice is very like, very. But, if you are my son, you can tell me where your mother is. Ha! ha! you can tell me that.

JOE. She is dead!

THORN. Dead! – who killed her? It must have been very sudden. Ah! I know; it was a blow – a heavy one; and her last words are now ringing in my ears: "Live and repent!" Ha! ha! but no one knows who dealt that blow, eh?

JOE. The hand I now grasp.

THORN. Me! Why, she has spoken a thousand times with pride, that I never raised my hand against her; the whole world knew that. Ah! (*with a sudden burst*) – oh! yes – I did. It was this hand, and it grasped the instrument of destruction—mine. Oh! what a scream, and what a horrid cry rings through the streets in the dark night. It is murder! Ha, ha! and they say the husband has killed his wife; and so he did—so he did. Look at the red stains around; look! it flows like a river; it creeps up to my feet; take me from it, or I shall perish in that dark sea Closer yet. And, oh! what a face is that glaring full upon me from the crimson pool! It is her's—Ruth's; I know it. She tells me I have murdered her, and a thousand voices echo it. And what is that by her side? It is the weapon of death; and a grinning fiend rises from the vapour, and mocks and points. It is the bottle! and the spirit of evil now madly laughs at its victim. Closer and closer yet. Oh! take me out—take me—(*sinks exhausted*)

JOE. Sister, go and take off your finery, I see the end of all this. I'll go back to my rags; honesty lasts, but these betray. Spurn all temptation, for here is a warning—a bitter lesson. I was half a thief, but this has changed me. Good-bye, father.

Enter GEORGE, *followed by* KEEPER.

KEEPER. You'll find him there. 'Tis nearly time for visitors to depart; take your farewell; for many days will elapse before you see him again. (*retires*)

GEORGE. Do you not remember me? (*advances to* THORNLEY)

THORN. I tell you, I know nothing; never had—Oh! ah! yes, I had a home, and there was a bright face there, ever beaming with smiles; children too, who loved. Where are they all? where is she? Gone! No more of the bitter scorn for her. I know where she is, that kind and loving mother; I'll tell you—there, there! Clouds open above me, and all is bright beyond. I see her sweet face looking faintly down upon me, but it is not the same smile of former days, for it is cold and angered; *but she is there!* Her spirit has fled to heaven; but the children, I left them last in rags—what, what will be their fate? No hope for them, none.

GEORGE. Yes, they shall be my care; I will find them a home—I will protect them.

THORN. You! Who are you that offers this?

GEORGE. A friend, who stretches forth a humble willing but a hand to snatch them from impending vice.

THORN. A friend—a friend to me! Why, who is this? The wretched have no friends—I found it so. Oh! I must know more of you—Oh! oh! I must!

KEEPER. His mad fit is coming on; you must part company now.

THORN. Part! who spoke of parting? No, no, don't part us; I must have company; I care not be alone again; the red stream rises. What sudden burst of light was that? It was one momentary ray of reason—the truth. I killed her, and I am mad. The shroud of darkness is drawn aside. She is dead, and heeds not now my tears. Oh! friend—for I know you now—and you, my children, judge me not too sternly; I feel that I am fast dying; let me die here; but, oh! what hope is there for me! (*clinging to* CHILDREN)

GEORGE. Resignation. Pray for forgiveness there.

THORN. Your pitying face seems to say a contrite spirit may be remembered at the Throne of Mercy. Kneel, kneel with me, children; and may thy tears wash away a parent's sin!

GEORGE. (*affected*) Richard!

THORN. Hush! their lips are stirred in prayer—for me, for me! Fold your arms around me—closer yet. What mist is that which is falling? what bubbling is this next my heart? Pray on, pray on—the sound grows fainter—fainter—I die in prayer. (*falls back*)

Curtain.

Printed by Thomas Scott, Warwick Court, Holborn.

THE GIN-SHOP

A Serial Illustration

BY

GEORGE CRUIKSHANK

THE GIN-SHOP.

ILLUSTRATED BY

GEORGE CRUIKSHANK.

Reprinted from the *Band of Hope Review*. An Illustrated Paper for the Young. Published Monthly. Price One Halfpenny.

This is the *Gin-shop* so glittering and gay.

There are the *Drinks* that are sold night and day,
At the bar of the Gin-shop, so glittering and gay.

There are the *Customers*, youthful and old,
Who drink the strong drinks which are sold night and day,
At the bar of the Gin-shop, so glittering and gay.

There is the *Landlord* who reaps the bright gold,
Out of the ruin of youthful and old,
Who drink the strong liquors he sells night and day,
At the bar of the Gin-shop, so glittering and gay.

There is the *Lady*, all jewels and lace,
The wife of the landlord who reaps the bright gold,
Out of the ruin of youthful and old,
Who drink the strong liquors he sells night and day,
At the bar of the Gin-shop, so glittering and gay.

There is the *Drunkard*, in rags and disgrace,
Who is served by the lady, all jewels and lace,
The wife of the landlord who reaps the bright gold,
Out of the ruin of youthful and old,
Who drink the strong liquors he sells night and day,
At the bar of the Gin-shop, so glittering and gay.

There is the *Wife*, with woebegone face,
The wife of the drunkard, in rags and disgrace,
Who is served by the lady, all jewels and lace,
The wife of the landlord who reaps the bright gold,
Out of the ruin of youthful and old,
Who drink the strong liquors he sells night and day,
At the bar of the Gin-shop, so glittering and gay.

There is the *Pistry*, so tender and kind,
Who pitied the woman, with woebegone face,
The wife of the drunkard, in rags and disgrace,
Who is served by the lady, all jewels and lace,
The wife of the landlord who reaps the bright gold,
Out of the ruin of youthful and old,
Who drink the strong liquors he sells night and day,
At the bar of the Gin-shop, so glittering and gay.

This is the *Pledge*, the poor drunkard signed,
Which was brought by the pastor, so tender and kind,
Who pitied the woman, with woebegone face,
And her husband, the drunkard, in rags and disgrace,
Who was served by the lady, all jewels and lace,
The wife of the landlord who reaps the bright gold,
Out of the ruin of youthful and old,
Who drink the strong liquors he sells night and day,
At the bar of the Gin-shop, so glittering and gay.

This is the *Church*, in which, one Sabbath-day,
The once wretched drunkard and wife took their way,
Drawn there by the pastor, so loving and kind,
Who brought him the pledge which he joyfully signed,
The pastor who pitied the woman's sad case,
And her husband, the drunkard, in rags and disgrace,
Who was served by the lady, all jewels and lace,
The wife of the landlord who reaps the bright gold,
Out of the ruin of youthful and old,
Who drink the strong liquors he sells night and day,
At the bar of the Gin-shop, so glittering and gay.

This is the *Tree*, which the good pastor chose,
And the light on the roof of the drunkard arose,
As he sat in the church, to which, one Sabbath-day,
Along with his wife he had taken his way,
Drawn there by the pastor, so loving and kind,
Who brought him the pledge which he joyfully signed,
The pastor who pitied the woman's sad case,
And her husband, the drunkard, in rags and disgrace,
Who was served by the lady, all jewels and lace,
The wife of the landlord who reaps the bright gold,
Out of the ruin of youthful and old,
Who drink the strong liquors he sells night and day,
At the bar of the Gin-shop, so glittering and gay.

This is the *College*, the home of delight,
Whence prayer, like an incense, ascends by night,
Where joy and contentment sit smiling so bright,—
Whence came this glad home where each comfort unites?
From the bottom that was wreck, the garret—these,
Where light on the roof of the drunkard arose,
As he sat in the church, to which, one Sabbath-day,
His wife and he, happy in heart, took their way,
Drawn there by the pastor, so tender and true,
Out of the pit sunk, an outcast and foul,
Who brought him the pledge which he joyfully signed,
The pastor who pitied the woman's sad case,
And her husband, the drunkard, in rags and disgrace,
Who was served by the lady, all jewels and lace,
The wife of the landlord who reaps the bright gold,
Out of the ruin of youthful and old,
Who drink the strong liquors he sells night and day,
At the bar of the Gin-shop, so glittering and gay.

Illustrated Wall-Paper.—Packet 3d.—No. 14. Price One Penny.   S. W. PARTRIDGE & CO., "BRITISH WORKMAN" OFFICE, 9, PATERNOSTER ROW, LONDON.

THIS is the *Gin-shop* all glittering and gay.

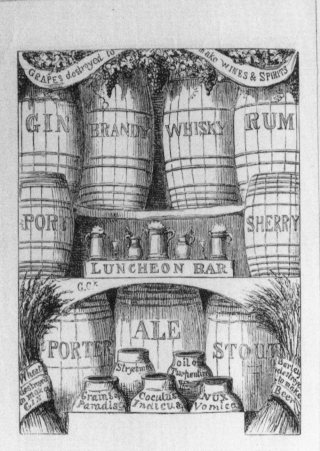

THESE are the *Drinks* that are sold night and day,
At the bar of the Gin-shop, so glittering and gay.

THESE are the *Customers*, youthful and old,
Who drink the strong drinks which are sold night and
day,
At the bar of the Gin-shop, so glittering and gay.

THIS is the *Landlord* who coins his bright gold,

Out of the ruin of youthful and old,

Who drink the strong liquors he sells night and day,

At the bar of the Gin-shop, so glittering and gay.

THIS is the *Lady*, all jewels and lace,
The wife of the landlord who coins his bright gold,
Out of the ruin of youthful and old,
Who drink the strong liquors he sells night and day,
At the bar of the Gin-shop, so glittering and gay.

THIS is the *Drunkard*, in rags and disgrace,
Who is served by the lady, all jewels and lace,
The wife of the landlord who coins his bright gold,
Out of the ruin of youthful and old,
Who drink the strong liquors he sells night and day,
At the bar of the Gin-shop, so glittering and gay.

THIS is the *Woman*, with wobegone face,
The wife of the drunkard, in rags and disgrace,
Who is served by the lady, all jewels and lace,
The wife of the landlord who coins his bright gold,
Out of the ruin of youthful and old,
Who drink the strong liquors he sells night and day,
At the bar of the Gin-shop, so glittering and gay.

THIS is the *Pastor*, so noble and kind,
Who pitied the woman, with wobegone face,
And the husband, the drunkard, in rags and disgrace,
Who is served by the lady, all jewels and lace,
The wife of the landlord who coins his bright gold,
Out of the ruin of youthful and old,
Who drink the strong liquors he sells night and day,
At the bar of the Gin-shop, so glittering and gay.

This is the *Paper*, the poor drunkard signed,
Which was brought by the pastor, so noble and kind,
Who pitied the woman, with wobegone face,
And her husband, the drunkard, in rags and disgrace;
Who was served by the lady, all jewels and lace,
The wife of the landlord who coins his bright gold,
Out of the ruin of youthful and old,
Who drink the strong liquors he sells night and day,
At the bar of the Gin-shop, so glittering and gay.

This is the *Church*, to which, one Sabbath-day,
The once wretched drunkard and wife took their way,
Drawn there by the pastor, so loving and kind,
Who brought him the pledge which he joyfully signed ;
The pastor who pitied the woman's sad case,
And her husband, the drunkard, in rags and disgrace ;
Who was served by the lady, all jewels and lace,
The wife of the landlord who coins his bright gold,
Out of the ruin of youthful and old,
Who drink the strong liquors he sells night and day,
At the bar of the Gin-shop, so glittering and gay.

"The Son of Man is come to seek and to save that which was lost."—LUKE xix.10.

This is the *Text*, which the good pastor chose,
And the light on the soul of the drunkard arose,
As he sat in the church, to which, one Sabbath-day,
Along with his wife he had taken his way,
Drawn there by the pastor, so loving and kind,
Who brought him the pledge which he joyfully signed;
The pastor who pitied the woman's sad case,
And her husband, the drunkard, in rags and disgrace;
Who was served by the lady, all jewels and lace,
The wife of the landlord who coins his bright gold,
Out of the ruin of youthful and old,
Who drink the strong liquors he sells night and day,
At the bar of the Gin-shop, so glittering and gay.

This is the *Cottage*, the home of delight,
Whence prayer, like an incense, ascends day and night,
Where joy and contentment sit smiling so bright—
Whence came this glad home where such comforts unite?
From the heaven-blest text which the pastor chose,
When light on the soul of the drunkard arose,
As he sat in the church, to which, each Sabbath-day,
His wife and he, happy at heart, take their way,
Drawn there by the pastor, so noble and kind,
Who brought him the pledge which he joyfully signed;
The pastor who pitied the woman's sad case,
And her husband, the drunkard, in rags and disgrace;
Who was served by the lady, all jewels and lace,
The wife of the landlord who coins his bright gold,
Out of the ruin of youthful and old,
Who drink the strong liquors he sells night and day,
At the bar of the Gin-shop, so glittering and gay.

PLATFORM PEARLS; OR, 19th CENTURY AMERICAN TEMPERANCE PERFORMANCE TEXTS

by Barbara Cohen-Stratyner

Temperance performance texts were created to inspire, convince and motivate their audiences. In the early decades of the secular temperance movement, when it shared followers and writers with the Abolitionist cause, the texts were designed to enforce the concept of alcohol usage as a form of social enslavement. After the Civil War, many adherents of the temperance cause promoted it as a solution to the destruction of the family by alcoholic men resulting in poverty, hopelessness and the need for children to work.

Throughout the century, temperance organizations and individual believers used a variety of text formats to promote their cause. This article and the bibliographies that follow resulted from research for the exhibition, *Temperance Hymns and Prohibition Parodies*, developed for The New York Public Library for the Performing Arts in the Spring of 1989. Materials in the exhibition were from the James Black Temperance Collection, General Research Division, The New York Public Library; and the Music Division and Billy Rose Theatre Collection, The New York Public Library for the Performing Arts, as well as the Library of Congress. Most collections of 19th century popular literature in areas with strong temperance affiliations will contain large numbers of listed texts. The bibliographies printed here focus on two kinds of interrelated performance texts – full-evening dramas printed as play series or prompt scripts, and short dialogues and recitations compiled into volumes. They share themes, approaches and often characters with prose writings and songs,

BARBARA COHEN-STRATYNER is the Curator of Exhibitions, The New York Public Library for the Performing Arts. She teaches at the Parsons School of Design and the City University of New York.

whether published with musical notations or with lyrics only printed as a broadside poem.

The power of these texts lay in their ability to combine the persuasive techniques of performance with the messages of temperance. The most successful focused on drinking as the destroyer of families with a rhetorical finesse perfected in 19th century melodramas and admonitory fiction. The conveyors of these messages in performance were women and children, socially and legally powerless against the evils of alcohol. The narrative voices embodied the power that the audience lacked.

The most optimistic temperance texts set their plot lines at the point of rejection of alcoholism. They gave advice to women urging them to use their moral influence to make their husbands, sons and male friends promise to remain abstinent. "Taking the Pledge" became a frequent theme in performance texts and fiction. Most readers will remember that "Laurie" took the pledge at "Meg's" wedding in *Little Women* while still only a social drinker. Most Pledge texts deal with drunkards, including the 1860 broadside, *Dear Father, drink no more*, which climaxes in a dramatic parental Pledge-taking:

> . . . Thus spake with tenderness the child;
> The drunkard's heart was mov'd.
> He sign'd the Pledge! He wept! He smil'd!
> And kissed the boy he lov'd.[1]

A female version set at a temperance meeting can be found in *Sign the Pledge for Mother's Sake*, written by Mrs. E. A. Parkhurst for her daughter "Little Effie Parkhurst at the great temperance gatherings in New-York and Boston:"

> Father dear I watch'd and waited knowing you would come at
>   last
> Tho' the tears I could not hinder and my heart was beating
>   fast!
> Now you're in this Temp'rance Meeting where your name
>   they'll gladly take,
> Will you, will you dearest father
> Sign the Pledge for mother's sake![2]

Performance texts for male voices could also narrate decisions on abstinence. One of the most popular was the stirring *The Soldier's song on Having Signed the Pledge*, published originally by the Antitobacco tract depository, Fitchburg, Massachusetts, 1850. *The Dying Drunkard*, written and performed by Sam Hotalin in the 1860s, was a death scene:

... A drink! A drink! he hoarsely cried; Once more before I'm
    dead

But the hand of death was in that room Upon that drunkard's
    bed ...

With tottering steps, his wife drew near, and breathed for
    him a prayer.

His heart was touched, he clasped her hand, And called his
    children there;

Oh Allie dear! I've wronged you all, Forgive me all I've said.

And tears of joy bedimmed her eye, As she wept by that
    drunkard's bed ...

A peaceful smile was on his face; He'd repented all he'd done
    and said.

A vision flitted before his eye And left that drunkard – dead!

since, years have passed; but memory's left on many a
    widow's head

A scene like this in every land of a dying Drunkard's bed.[3]

"Pledge" texts could also be satiric. A stricture, such as "Don't
Marry a Drinking Man," might be presented as a song and broadside,
like Mrs. E. A. Parkhurst's *Don't Marry a Man if He Drinks*, a drama,
such as Harry Seymour's *Aunt Dinah's Pledge*, a dialogue, such as
Nellie H. Bradley's *Laura's Plan and how it succeeded*, and a platform
speech. Each of these might then generate answer texts, such as
Parkhurst's popular songs *Girls, Wait for a Temperance Man*, and *I'll
Marry No Man if He Drinks*. They inspire and shock the young
women in the audience by using explicit contemporary details. Lis-
teners to the former song might sniff their fiance's breath after hear-
ing the advising narrator describe "Young men who are given to
bitters:"

... They feel quite at home on the corners,

They vote the Excise Tax a bore;

And they've plenty of cloves in their pockets,

    when they visit the girl they adore.[4]

There was a very real danger to women and children from alcoholic
consumption by men. In a period in which women had few property
rights, they could easily be ruined by someone else's expenditures.
Admonitory songs, broadsides, plays and dialogues were therefore
both popular and persuasive. The plays based on George Cruikshank
illustrations are among the best known examples of admonitory
pledge dramas and Taylor's melodrama, *The Bottle*, and Cruikshanks'
The Gin-Shop are reproduced in full below.

There were many admonitory texts with adult narrative voices that

presented the financial and social impact of another's drinking. The
Hutchinson Family, best remembered for the Abolitionist songs, featured temperance ballads in their repertory, among them "The
Lament of the Widowed Inebriate."[5] Most temperance dramas, from
the most famous *Ten Nights in a Barroom* to obscure terror-filled
plots such as *Ruined by drink, The wages of sin, The fruits of the wine
cup* and *Adrift*, destroyed entire families in three to five act melodramas to show the influence of drinking on society.

Plotted ballads printed with music or as broadsides used single
narrative voices to represent the family and society. The mother's
narrative voice was popular in song texts. Charles H. Gabriel, America's foremost Gospel hymnist, wrote one of the classic ballads of
mother love and redemption for the temperance movement, *He's a
Drunkard Tonight.*

> Somewhere tonight in this cold dreary world,
> Wanders a boy that I cherish so,
> Reading the dark and unbidden road, leading to misery, pain
>   and woe.
> Gentle and true, not a sin to blight,
> When but a boy he was my delight.
> Pure as the snow and as spotless white,
> Yet, Oh God, he's a drunkard tonight.[6]

Admonitory performance texts could also focus their moral
example on fictional children – orphans, beggars, street sellers, and
the homeless, who had suffered because alcohol destroyed their families. This tactic, derived from the personalized editorials of 19th century journalism, is still in use in donation request literature, the so-
called "beg letters" that we all receive. These plots ended with the
death of the child and were designed to terrify drinking men and
women into abstinence to save their families.

Many individual characters, such as "Little Mary Morgan," "Little
Bessie" and "Little Katy," appear in novels, songs, broadsides and
dramatizations by different authors. We can cynically explain the
presence of these young girls in plays, since so many of the travelling
theatre companies had a suitable child on hand to play "Little Eva" in
Uncle Tom's Cabin. But the pervasive presence of so many such characters in so many forms of performance texts must reveal the genuine
impact of that narrative voice.

"Little Mary Morgan" was the child victim in dramatizations of
Timothy Shay Arthur's 1858 novel, *Ten Nights in a Barroom.* The
most famous of these was by William W. Pratt in the 1860s and
starred the original "Little Eva," Cordelia Howard. Versions of the
play and slide lectures based directly on the novel abounded through-

out the latter half of the 19th century.[7] In the sequence followed by most versions, Mary is sent to the barroom to fetch her father on the Second Night and is injured by the glass thrown by the tavern keeper at her father. On the Third Night, her fever from the head wound is compared to her father's delirium tremens. She dies on the Fourth Night, as her father promises to take the Pledge. He returns on the Tenth Night as a temperance lecturer. Although she never actually says "Father, dear Father, come home with me now" in the Arthur or Pratt versions, it became the character's trademark. Henry Clay Work's song *Come home Father*, features that line in its chorus.

"Mary" became prevalent as the name of "the drunkard's poor child" soon after 1860, most probably in an effort to cash in on the widespread popularity of the novel. The typical 1860 broadside, *Oh! Help little Mary, the drunkard's poor child*, does not reproduce the plot of the novel, but does reflect its situation – a child urging abstinence:

> Now will you oh friends, you with hearts kind and warm
> Will you help the dear Father I love to reform.
> For my sad heart sometimes with sorrow grows wild.
> Oh help little Mary, the drunkard's poor child.[8]

"Little Bessie" occurs in songs, dialogues and broadsides in the 1860s. The phrase "Father's a drunkard and mother is dead" appears in each. It cannot at this time be determined which version contained the original character and which were the imitations, but the text published both as *Drunkard's Lone Child* and *Father's a Drunkard and Mother is Dead* seems to be the most popularly known. In it, "Bessie" ranges from piteous to politicized as she requests assistance from temperance workers in a child's dialect voice:

> We were so happy till father drank rum
> Then all our sorrows and troubles begun,
> Mother grew paler and wept every day,
> Baby and I were too hungry to play.
> Slowly they faded and one summer night,
> Found their sweet faces all silent and white,
> And with big tears slowly dropping, I said,
> Father's a drunkard and mother is dead.
> Chorus: – Mother, oh, why did you leave me alone
>   With no one to love me, no friends and no home,
>   Dark is the night, and the storm rages wild,
>   God pity Bessie, the Drunkard's Lone Child.
>   Oh, if the temp'rancemen only could find
>   Poor wretched Father and talk very kind,
>   If they could stop him from drinking, why then

I should be so very happy again!
Is it too late? Men of Temp'rance, please try
Or poor little Bessie may soon starve and die . . .[9]

The case of "Little Katy" shows the power of the image of the child victim. "Little Katy" was invented by Horace Greeley as the personification of the New York slums in an editorial in the *New York Tribune*. The child, a street seller of hot corn, lived in the Five Points area of lower New York and her forced labor represented, for Greeley, one of the worst evils of alcoholism.[10] Solon Robinson turned the editorial into a novel, *Hot Corn, Life Scenes in New York*, published in 1854 and then wrote a dramatization. Its plot and characters were used by John E. Durviage in his unpublished dramatization later that year for performances at the Bowery Theatre.[11] Soon, "Little Katy" songs and broadsides flooded the market. Most gave the Greeley editorial as their direct source. *Little Katy, or Hot Corn*, by James Simmons and Quos for Wood's Minstrels (New York: Horace Waters, 1853), stated that it was "suggested to Mr. Wood by the beautiful and effecting story of the same name as published in the *New York Tribune*, August 5th." *Katy's Cry "Come Buy My Hot Corn"*, a different song also published by Horace Waters for Wood's Minstrels, was "written for the benefit of the House of Industry . . . by permission dedicated to Horace Greeley, Esq . . . the profit derived from the sale of this song will be given to that admirable institution, one of the best of all charities, entitled the Five Points House of Industry."[12]

The generic child characters who appear in multiple performance texts lack names, but share a history of abuse and poverty. These texts include both tragic descriptions of conditions and explicit requests for abstinence. The narrative voice was almost always female since young fictional girls were deemed best at declaiming emotion. When a child died within the text, however, it was almost always male, like the unnamed son in *Sign the Pledge for Mother's Sake* and the child in *Dear Father Come Home*:

Oh! mother, oh mother, dear father's come home,
he knows little Benny is dead;
with agony weeping, he's breaking his heart,
he seems to be out of his head;
His thoughts now are on our poor Benny that's gone,
his form appears always in sight –
and he keeps on repeating the last words he said,
"I want to kiss Papa good night."[13]

Example of pathos abound in broadsides such as *Come Home, Father* (ca. 1858), *Father, Bring Home Your Money Tonight* and *Poor Drunkard's Child*:

> How shrill is the tempest that rattle without
> and I am near frozen within.
> The house is so lonesome and dreary and dark
> For Father's drinking again.[14]

A similar ballad by Dr. T. H. Peacock, an avid temperance propagandist in prose and song, was more explicit in its description of the abuse:

> Yes Father's been drinking and beat Mother so
> I tried hard to save her the terrible blow;
> But struck to the floor—she there senseless lay,
> For trying to save her—he drove me away.
> Then please sir, go with me, I dare not go there,
> And Mother, so wretched, deep sunk in despair,
> And all is Rum's doing, —once happy were we,
> And all laughed and sang in our innocent glee.[15]

The politicized child demanding temperance and abstinence occurs most often in dramatizations as a stage conflict between the drunken father (generally the star character actor) and the pathetic child. Many of the dialogues by Nellie H. Bradley, Lizzie Penney and their anonymous colleagues train their child readers to confront their drinking parents. One broadside in which the un-named narrator directed pleas and demands at her father was *Drunkard's Child*:

> Once we were so happy and we had bread to eat,
> And mamma and I were warmly clad and life seemed very
>   sweet;
> You never spoke unkindly then, or dealt with anger blow
> O, father dear, 'tis sad to see
> That drink has changed you so.[16]

Little Pleader, a ballad by Florence Brightly and Dr. Peacock, is typical of a dramatized narrative song on this subject. The narrative voice belongs to the child for four verses and choruses of pleading. The father, to whom it is aimed, repents in the final verse:

> quickly bending kissed his child,
> Yes, little one, I'll stay.[17]

As temperance organizations gained political power, many became less secular. Affiliations with evangelist movements of the late 19th and early 20th century led to a de-emphasis on theatre presentations.

The persuasive power of *The Bottle, Ten Nights in a Bar-Room* and *The Drunkard* was lost as temperance groups joined with those favoring Blue Laws against theatres and Sunday performances. Music, which was not banned in Blue Law municipalities, became the prime purveyor of the Temperance message through hymns and anthems by such popular Revival composers as Charles H. Gabriel and Homer Rodeheaver. Although many historians believe that the merging of the Temperance and evangelist movements was a major factor in the eventual success of state and federal legislation prohibiting alcohol manufacture, distribution and use, it ended the wide-spread creation and promotion of persuasive performance texts.

ENDNOTES:

[1] Americana Collection, Music Division, The New York Public Library for the Performing Arts. (hereafter Music Divison, NYPL)

[2] *Sign the Pledge . . .*, word by Mrs. M. A. Kidder, music by Mrs. E. A. Parkhurst. New York: Wm. A. Pond & Co., 1857. Music Division, Library of Congress.

[3] Music Division, NYPL.

[4] New York: C. M. Tremaine, 1867. Music Division, NYPL.

[5] Published in *The Granite Songster*. (Boston: A. B. Hutchinson, 1847).

[6] Chicago: E. O. Excell, 1889. Music Division, Library of Congress. Gabriel's compositions include such Gospel and Country & Western standards as *His Eye is on the Sparrow* and *Will the Circle Be Unbroken*.

[7] See William M. Clark, "Ten Nights in a Barroom," *American Heritage*, Vol. 15, No. 4 (June 1964), pp. 14–17, for an analysis of the slide lectures.

[8] *Oh Help little Mary*, is considered an anonymous broadside. A song with the same title is credited to Mrs. Parkhurst (as composer) on the cover of her *Sign the Pledge for Mother's Sake*.

[9] *Father's a Drunkard and Mother is Dead* is considered an anonymous broadside. A song with the same title is credited to Mrs. Parkhurst (as composer) on the cover of her *Sign the Pledge for Mother's Sake*.

[10] August 5, 1853.

[11] Program, Bowery Theatre, April 6, 1854. Theatres:US:NY:Bowery. Programs, Billy Rose Theatre Collection, The New York Public Library for the Performing Arts.

[12] *Little Katy* has words by James Simmonds and music by Quos. *Katy's Cry* has words by James Such and music by J. B. Woodbury and was published in 1858. Both songs and broadside versions of each can be found in the American Collection, Music Division, NYPL.

[13] *Dear Father's Come Home*, words by Gen. W. H. Hayward, music by J. T. Gosden. Baltimore: Henry McCaffrey, 1866.

[14]Anonymous, ca. 1860. Music Division, NYPL.

[15]*Pity Me Stranger*, words by F. A. Conly, music by Dr. Thos. H. Peacock. Copyright by Lee & Walker, 1872. Music Division, Library of Congress.

[16]Anonymous, Philadelphia: J. H. Johnson, Song Publisher, Stationer & Printer, 1871. Music Division, NYPL.

[17]Copyright by Lee & Walker, 1872. Music Division, Library of Congress.

BIBLIOGRAPHIES OF TEMPERANCE PERFORMANCE TEXTS

by Barbara Cohen-Stratyner

This bibliography is the result of research for the exhibition, *Temperance Hymns and Prohibition Parodies*, developed for The New York Public Library for the Performing Arts in 1990. The exhibition, included books, sheet music and illustrated broadsides of 19th century temperance performance texts and anti-Prohibition satires from Broadway revues. Temperance texts were printed in the many thousands for wide-spread distribution, so they can still be found in many libraries and historical collections. These bibliographies were compiled from materials in four different divisions of The New York Public Library: The James Black Temperance Collection, General Research Division; the Literature holdings of the General Research Division; the Billy Rose Theatre Collection, The New York Public Library for the Performing Arts; and the Americana Collection, Music Division, The New York Public Library for the Performing Arts. Neither the exhibition nor the bibliographies could have been completed without the assistance of Elizabeth Diefendorf, at the GRD, and of Jean Bowen and Richard Jackson at the Music Division.

Full titles have been reproduced in the bibliographies since they reveal both the content and the targeted audience of the volumes. Even a brief look at the listings shows the importance of institutional publishing to the temperance cause. Many of the performance texts were printed by such organizations as The National Temperance Society and Publication House, the American Temperance Union, and the Woman's Temperance Publications Association – groups that could guarantee distribution to an avid, pre-persuaded audience. Other works were printed by commercial publishers such as Funk & Wagnalls and Dick & Fitzgerald, but were sponsored by and sold to the membership groups listed in their titles. Volumes aimed at the Washingtonians, the Bands of Hope, White Ribbons Army, Blue Button Army and the children's Cold Water Army can all be found in the performance text bibliographies.

Dialogues, Exercises and Recitations

Many volumes of dialogues, exercises and recitations were published with some form of musical notation, ranging from solfege to letter or numerical texts. Those volumes with conventional piano-vocal music notation are marked with an asteric (*).

Anon. *The Band of Hope songster; a collection of appropriate songs for Band of Hope and other juvenile temperance meetings. Boston: Stacy & Adams, 1859.

Anon. The Cold Water [Army] melodies, and Washington songster. Boston: T. Abbot, 1842.

Anon. *Crystal Fount; containing hymns, rounds, moral & temperance songs [for] juvenile abstinence meetings. New York: P. J. Cozans, 1860.

Anon. The Sunday-school concert. A collection of twenty-six concert exercises and dialogues. New York: The National Temperance Society and Publication House, 1881.

Anon. Temperance anecdotes and interesting facts. Boston: G. W. Light, 1834.

Anon. Temperance dialogue . . . for three boys and a girl. New York: [DeWitt's School Dialogue], 187–.

Anon. Temperance fables, for the American people. New York: Brogard & Co., 1850.

Anon. *The Temperance minstrel. A collection of songs for temperance societies, &c. Detroit: Bagg and Harmon, 1847.

Anon. The Temperance school dialogues. A collection of dramatic and effective dialogues calculated to show the evil of intemperance; designed for the use of temperance societies, district lodges and all interested in temperance. New York: DeWitt's School Dialogues, no. 15, H. J. Wehman, 1892.

Anon. *Temperance songs. Philadelphia: J. H. Jackson, 186–.

Anon. The Temperance text-book: a collection of facts and interesting anecdotes, illustrating the evil of intoxicating drinks. Philadelphia: E. L. Carey and A. Hart, 1836.

Anon. [A Friend to Temperance] The Evils of intemperance, exemplified in poetry and prose. Boston: N. Boynton, 1829.

Anon. [The Voice] Songs for the new crusade; selected prohibition and

Prohibition Party songs sent in competition for a prize offered by "The Voice." New York: Funk & Wagnalls, 1887.

Adlington, Francis Morse. **The fountain minstrel; or, Tee-totaller's new song-book. Calculated to be used at temperance meetings, pic-nics, etc.* Boston: B. Marsh, 1846.

Aikman, James H. **The Washingtonian harp, a collection of original songs adapted to familiar airs and arranged to be sung either as solos or choruses designed for the use of the Washington temperance societies.* New York: Burnett & Allen, 1842; New-York: Saxton and Miles, 1843.

Ames, Julia A. *Platform voices.* Chicago: Woman's Temperance Publications Association, 1887.

Baker, George Melville. *The temperance drama; a series of dramas, comedies, and farces, for temperance exhibitions and home and school entertainment,* Boston: Lee and Shepard and New York: Lee, Shepard and Dillingham, 1874.

Bechtel, J. H., Ed. *Temperance selections, comprising choice readings and recitations in prose and verse from the ablest speakers and writers in England and America.* Philadelphia: Penn Publishing Co., 1913.

Bensel, Abraham. *The temperance harp, containing firemen's and other songs . . . designed for the use of temperance societies, meetings and concerts throughout the Union.* New York: Burnett & Allen, 1842.

Blood, Mary E. *The triple pledge. A Temperance concert exercise for Sunday-schools.* New York: The National Temperance Society and Publication House, 1888.

Bradbury, William Batchelder. *Temperance chimes; comprising a great variety of new music, glees, songs, and hymns, designed for the use of temperance meetings and organizations, glee clubs, bands of hope, and the home circle; together with the odes of the order of the Sons of Temperance and Good templars.* New York: The National Temperance Society and Publication House, 1887.

Bradley, Nellie H. *New Temperance dialogues.* Rockland, Maine: Z. P. Vose & Co., 1868, including
The first glass; or, The power of woman's influence;
Marry no man if he drinks; or, Laura's plan and how it succeeded.
Reclaimed; or, The danger of moderate drinking.
The young teetotaler; or, Saved at last;
_____. *New Temperance dialogues. The stumbling block; or, Why a deacon gave up his wine.* Rockland, Maine: Z. P. Vose & Co., 1871.
_____. *New Temperance dialogues. Wine as a medicine; or, Abbie's experiment.* Rockland, Maine: Z. P. Zose & Co., 1873.

_____. *A Temperance picnic, with, the old woman who lived in a shoe. New York: The National Temperance Society and Publication House, 1888.

Burleigh, William H. *Poems.* New York: Hurd & Houghton, 1871.

_____. *The rum fiend, and other poems.* New York: The National Temperance Society and Publication House, 1871.

Cary, S. F., Ed. *The national Temperance offering; and Sons and Daughters of Temperance gift.* New York: R. Vandien, 1850.

Clark, Edmund. *Temperance exercise. A Sabbath-school concert exercise.* Rockland, Maine: Z. P. Vose & Co., 1872.

Colman, Julia. *An evening with Robinson Crusoe . . . in six parts.* New York: The National Temperance Society and Publication House, 1891.

_____. *No king in America. A patriotic temperance programme in three parts.* New York: The National Temperance Society and Publication House, 1888.

_____. *Readings on Beer.* New York: The National Temperance Society and Publication House, 1887.

_____. *Readings on Cider.* New York: The National Temperance Society and Publication House, 1887.

Denison, Thomas Stewart. *Hard cider; a temperance sketch.* Chicago: T. S. Denison, 1880.

Dietz, Mrs. William H., compiler. *Graded temperance helps. containing temperance mottoes, songs, recitations, stories and illustrative exercises.* Chicago: W. H. Dietz, nd.

Dunn, James C. *Band of Hope manual; containing directions how to form Bands of Hope; also, constitutions for Bands of Hope and Bands of Hope ritual, together with dialogues, recitations, hymns, etc.* New York: The National Temperance Society and Publication House, 1867; 1869.

Erickson, Matilda. *Temperance torchlights . . . studies, stories, songs, poems, and useful information on temperance topics; for the use of individuals, churches, schools, temperance and young people's societies.* Washington, D.C.: Review and Herald Publication Association, 1910.

Gordon, Anna Adams. *Marching songs for young crusaders. Temperance songs for the cold water army.* Chicago: Woman's Temperance Publications Association, 1881. nb: reprinted often for the next 40 years. After 1904, the publisher was Evanston, Ill.: National Women's Christian Temperance Union.

_____. *Prohibiton program for the use of juvenile temperance societies, including songs, recitations and exercises for an evening's entertainment* Chicago: Woman's Temperance Publications Association, 188-.

_____. *The White Ribbon Birthday Book*. Chicago: Woman's Temperance Publications Association, 1887.

Grosh, Aaron Burt. *Temperance pocket companion; containing a choice collection of temperance hymns, songs, odes, glees, duets, choruses, etc.* Utica, N.Y.: B. S. Merrell, 1852.

_____. *Washingtonian pocket companion; containing a choice collection of temperance hymns, songs, odes, glees, duets, choruses, etc.* Utica, N.Y.: B. S. Merrell, Roberts & Curtiss, 1843; B. S. Merrill, 1845.

Guernsey, Alice Margaret. *Program for an entertainment in behalf of the temperance temple*. Chicago: Woman's Temperance Publications Association, 1888.

_____. *Program for an entertainment on scientific temperance instruction*. Chicago: Woman's Temperance Publications Association, 1887.

Hadley, Henry Harrison. *The blue badge of courage*. Akron, Ohio: The Saalfield Publishing Co., 1902.

Hammond, S. T. *A collection of temperance dialogues for Divisions of Sons, Good Templar lodges, Sections of cadets, Bands of Hope, and other temperance societies*. Ottawa: S. T. Hammond, 1869.

Hart, Lucius, compiler. *The juvenile temperance harp, consisting of chorus songs, duetts, glees, sacred and temperance melodies. Especially adapted for meetings of the American Juvenile Temperance Society and other juvenile associations*. New York: J. B. Dunn, 1857.

Herbert, Sidney. *The young volunteer campaign melodist. Designed for the use of Bands of Hope and all other juvenile reform organizations*. Boston: J. M. Usher, 1864.

Hubbard, Stephen. *The new temperance melodist; consisting of glees, songs and pieces, composed and arranged for the use of the various temperance organizations in the United States and Canada*. Boston: Oliver Ditson & Co., 1859; Boston: J. P. Jewett and Co., 1859.

_____. *The temperance melodist; consisting of glees, songs and pieces, arranged and adapted expressly for the use of "Temperance Watchmen," "Sons of Temperance," societies, temperance gatherings, and for social and family circles throughout the union*. Boston: Kidder & Cheever, 1852.

Hull, Asa. *Hull's Temperance glee book, containing a choice variety of temperance songs, duets and choruses suitable for the sociable entertainments of the several temperance organizations . . .* Boston: Oliver Ditson & Co., 1877.

Hutchinson Family. *The Book of Words of the Hutchinson Family*. Boston: J. S. Potter & Co., 1855.

_____. *The Granite Songster.* Boston: A. B. Hutchinson, 1847.

Jewitt, Charles. *The Youth's Temperance Lecturer.* Boston: Whipple and Damrell, 1840.

Kemp, "Mother." *The Fanueil Hall temperance song book.* Boston: Press of S. G. Jones & Co., 1876.

Knorr, James. *The two roads; or, The right and the wrong.* Philadelphia: Lippincott, Orambo & Co., 1854.

Leonard, Silas W. and J. Young. *The national temperance songster.* Louisville, Kentucky: Morton & Griswold, 1854.

Marsh, John. *A Boy's Temperance book.* New York: American Temperance Union, 1848.

_____. *Marsh's temperance anecdotes. A choice collection of more than two hundred temperance anecdotes accumulating through twenty years, illustrating the evils of intemperance and the power of the pledge . . . useful to temperance lecturers.* New York: American Temperance Union, 1848.

_____. *Roll and exercise book for the Banks of hope . . .* New York: American Temperance Union, 1862.

_____. *The temperance speaker, compiled from various sources.* New York: American Temperance Union, 1860; 1868.

Mather, Mary H. *Ye hatchet partie and other entertainments.* Chicago: Women's Temperance Publication Association, 1869.

McBride, H. Elliot. *A bitter doze.* New York: The National Temperance Society and Publications House, 1878.

_____. *A boy's rehearsal.* New York: The National Temperance Society and Publication House, 1879.

_____. *The poisoned darkies; a temperance interlude in one act for male characters only.* New York: Dick & Fitzgerald, 1877.

_____. *A talk on temperance.* New York: The National Temperance Society and Publication House, 1879.

_____. *Temperance dialogues, designed for the use of schools, temperance societies, Bands of Hope. . . .* New York: Dick & Fitzgerald, 1888.

_____. *Well fixed for a rainy day. A temperance play in one act . . . with the cast of characters, costumes. . . .* New York: Dick & Fitzgerald, 1882.

McDermott, J. J. *A game of billiards. A temperance sketch in one scene.* New York: Happy Hours Company, 1875.

Moffitt, W. G. *God speed the right. The national temperance songster . . . a collection of fresh and sparkling original temperance songs.* Indianapolis: S. L. Morrow & Co., 1879.

Morse, Mrs. E. L. *The drunkard's journey, a Sunday school concert exercise.* Boston: Congregational Publication Society, 1870.

Mowatt, James Alexander. *Mowatt's temperance glee book*. New York: Hubbard & Munro, 1874.

Newton, Alonzo Elliot, compiler. *Manual of the Ganguard of Freedom ... with hymns, songs, recitations, and dialogues.* New York: The National Temperance Society and Publication House, 1867.

Penney, Lizzie, Ed. *A Christmas entertainment. A concert temperance exercise for Sunday-schools, Bands of Hope, juvenile temples, loyal temperance legions, etc., etc.* New York: The National Temperance Society and Publication House, 1874.

———. *Gems for Bands of Hope.* New York: The National Temperance Society and Publication House, 1895.

———. *The Juvenile Temperance reader. A collection of choice recitations and declamations in prose and verse.* New York: The National Temperance Society and Publication House, 1876.

———. *Rallying songs for young teetotalers. Designed for bands of hope, Sunday schools, juvenile temples, loyal legions, temperance schools and other juvenile societies.* New York: The National Temperance Society and Publication House, 1895.

———. *Readings and recitations. A new and choice collection of articles in prose and verse ...* New York: The National Temperance Society and Publication House, 1878.

———. *The Temperance platform. Orations on total abstinence and prohibition, especially adapted for prize contest, public meetings, social gatherings, etc.* New York: The National Temperance Society and Publication House, 1892.

———. *The Water Lily series.* New York: The National Temperance Society and Publication House, 1891, including
  Brave boys and girls
  Bright stories for young readers
  Little dew-drops
  Little drops of water
  Little people's favorites
  Pebbles and pearls
  Pebbles from the brook

Perkins, Theodore E., Ed. *The golden mean, a variety of new music, new songs and choice selections designed for the meetings of the Business-Men's Society for the Encouragement of Moderation, its auxiliary organizations and the home circle.* New York: Anderson & Co., 1879.

Plimpton, Job. *The Washingtonian choir ... songs, duets, trios, catches and choruses, original and selected. With an accompaniment for the piano-forte or organ. Composed, selected, arranged and adapted to the cause of total abstinence.* Boston: Kidder and Wright, 1843.

Potter, R. K., compiler. *The Boston temperance songster; a collection of songs and hymns for temperance societies. Boston: W. White, 1844.

Rogers, H. M. Ed. *Rogers' selection of moderation songs; also national, pathetic, sacred and descriptive songs and ballads. New York: Anderson & Co., 1870.

Root, George Frederick, compiler. *The musical fountain. Chicago: Root & Cady, 1866.

Sherwin, William Fisk *Bugle songs for the Temperance army. New York: The National Temperance Society and Publication House, 1871. Also published as Bugle notes . . .

Silver Lake Quartette [C. H. Mead and G. E. Chambers]. *The clarion call. For amendment campaigns, reform clubs, temperance organizations, and prohibition camps. New York: Funk & Wagnalls, 1889.

_____. *Prohibition bells and songs of the new crusade, for temperance organizations, reform clubs, prohibition camps, and political campaigns. New York: Funk & Wagnalls, 1888.

Stearns, John Newton, Ed. *Band of hope songster; a collection of temperance songs. Designed for bands of hope, Sunday-schools, juvenile temples, temperance schools and other juvenile societies. New York: The National Temperance Society and Publication House, 1889.

_____. *Constitutional amendment songster, for prohibition campaigns. New York: The National Temperance Society and Publication House, 1889.

_____. *National temperance hymn and song book. A new collection of popular temperance hymns and songs, for all temperance organizations. New York: The National Temperance Society and Publication House, 1880.

_____. *The prohibition songster . . . for prohibition campaign clubs, temperance organizations, glee clubs, camp-meetings, etc., etc. New York: The National Temperance Society and Publication House, 1885.

_____. *The Temperance hymn-book; a collection of choice songs and hymns adapted to familiar tunes, suitable for all temperance organizations, prayer-meetings, and social gatherings. New York: The National Temperance Society and Publication House, 1869.

_____. The Temperance speaker; a collection of original and selected dialogues, addresses, and recitations, for the use of temperance organizations, schools, bands of hope, anniversaries, etc. New York: The National Temperance Society and Publication House, 1869; 1871.

Tardy, Edwin. *Saved, A temperance sketch*. Clyde, Ohio: O. A. D. Ames, 188–. Ames' series of standard and minor drama, no. 59.

Tenney, John H. *Temperance jewels for temperance and reform meetings*. . . . Boston: Oliver Ditson, 1879.

Thayer, George. *The two ways. A Temperance concert exercise for Sunday-school, reform clubs, temperance organizations, etc.* New York: The National Temperance Society and Publication House, 1876.

Thompson, Edwin. *Thompson's Band of Hope melodies, consisting of temperance songs, duets and glees, especially adapted for Bands of Hope and other juvenile temperance associations.* Boston: Wright & Potter, 1864.

Thompson, Thomas R. *The contrast; a Temperance concert exercise.* New York: The National Temperance Society and Publication House, 1897.

Van Tassel, Truman. **Temperance odes. Designed for the use of temperance societies.* Seneca Fall, N.Y.: J. H. Child, 1835.

Wallace, William, Ed. **The Croton wreath, or Boston Washingtonian melodies.* Boston: C. H. Brainard, 1843.

Wheeler, L. May, compiler. *Booklet of song, a collection of suffrage and temperance melodies.* Minneapolis: Co-operative Printing Co., 1884.

White, Laura W. *A plea from the vegetable kingdom . . . for a class exercise by the Newtown First-day School, at the Friends' Temperance Meeting [August 10, 1886].* Newtown, Pennsylvania: Enterprise Steam Printing House, 1886.

Willard, Frances Elizabeth, compiler. *Recitation book.* New York: E. S. Werner Publishing and Supply Co., 1898.

Wright, Mrs. Julia McNair. *Mother Goose for temperance nurseries.* New York: The National Temperance Society and Publication House, 1872.

———. *A temperance arithmetic for school and families.* New York: The National Temperance Society and Publication House, 1889.

Young Temperance volunteers of Boston. *The Young volunteer campaign melodist.* Boston: for the Executive Committee by J. M. Usher, 1867.

Periodicals including dialogues, songs, etc. in most issues

The American Temperance magazine and Sons of Temperance offering. New York: H. Van Dien, 1850–1852.

The Crystal fount. National magazine for the Sons, Daughters and Cadets of Temperance, for the promotion of temperance, litera-

ture, science and religion. Baltimore: Williams, Smith & Co., 1847-1848.

The Family Favorite & Temperance journal. Adrian, Michigan, 1849-1850.

The National Advocate. New York: The National Temperance Society and Publication House, 1866-1906.

Temperance Lesson manual for the Band of Hope and Loyal Temperance Legion. Chicago: Woman's Temperance Publication Association, 1886.

Microform collections of temperance materials including dialogues, songs, etc.

History of Women. Microform materials in . . . Radcliffe College, Smith College, The New York Public Library, etc. New Haven, Connecticut: Research Publications, 1965-1979.

Jimerson, Randall C., Francis X. Blouin and Charles Isetts. *Guide to the microform edition of temperance and prohibition papers in . . . Michigan Historical Society, Ohio Historical Society and the Women's Christian Temperance Union*, Ann Arbor, Michigan: University of Michigan, 1977.

Taylor, Earl R. *Massachusetts temperance societies' publications: a bibliography of 19th century materials in the Boston Public Library, the American Antiquarian Society and the Massachusetts Historical Society.* New York: Garland Press, 1984.

Temperance Writings based on George Cruikshank illustrations

Anon. *The history of the bottle, as originally published in the New-York Organ.* New York: Oliver & Brother, 1848.

Anon. *The power of the pledge, a sequel to The bottle.* New York: Oliver & Brother, 1848.

Cruikshank, George. *The gin-shop.* London: S. W. Partridge, 1864; New York: The National Temperance Society and Publication House, 1876.

Hutchins, Benjamin F. *The gin-shop.* New York: The National Temperance Society and Publication House, 1883.

Pitt, Dibdin. *The bottle; or, the drunkard's doom.* Manchester: play-script, 1849.

Plunkett, Henry Grattan. *The bottle, a poem, suggested by the celebrated designs of Geo. Cruikshank.* New York: T. Watts, 1848.

Taylor, Tom. *The bottle; or, cause and effect.* New York: John

Douglas, 1847; London: T. H. Lacy, 1855; New York: Samuel French, 1877.

Watts, Talbot. *The drunkard's children; being the sequel to "The bottle;" a poem by H. P. Grattan, illustrating the celebrated designs of Geo. Cruikshank.* New York: T. Watts, 1849.

Evening-length dramas

Anon. *Stanhope; or, By hook or by crook!.* Ypsilanti, Michigan: The Band of hope, 1882.

Anon. *The power of the pledge, a sequel to The bottle.* New York: Oliver & Brother, 1848.

Adkisson, Noble. *Ruined by drink . . . in four acts.* New York: Samuel French, 1889. French's standard drama, no. 404.

———. *The wages of sin. A temperance drama in three acts.* Sulpher Springs, Texas: N. Adkisson, 1888.

Allen, John Allen. *The fruits of the wine cup; a drama . . . in three acts . . . With cast of characters, stage business, costumes [descriptions], relative positions, &c. [from 1858 production].* New York: Samuel French, 186-. French's standard drama, no. 354.

Babcock, Charles W. *Adrift. A temperance drama, in three acts . . . to which is added, a description of costumes, characters, entrances and exits; with the stage business carefully marked.* Clyde, Ohio: O. A. D. Ames, 1880. Ames' standard and minor drama, no. 75.

Baker, George Melville. *A drop too much.* Boston: Lee & Shepard, 1866.

———. *Handy dramas for amateur actors. New pieces for home, school and public entertainment,* including
  The flower of the family
  A mysterious disappearance
  The little brown jug &c.

———. *Past redemption.* Boston: Lee & Shepard, 1875. Baker's editions of plays.

Bradley, Nellie H. *Having fun.* New York: The National Temperance Society and Publications Association, 1883.

Brown, Charles P. and G. Tompkins. *A glass of wine; an emotional temperance drama in five acts.* Brooklyn: Brown & Tompkins, 1877.

Comstock, William. *Rum; or, the first glass. A drama in three acts.* New York: DeWitt, 1875.

Cook, S. N. *Broken promises . . . in five acts.* New York: Happy Hours Company, 1879.

Cutler, F. L. *Lost! Or, the fruits of the glass.* Clyde, Ohio: O. A. D. Ames, 1882. Ames' standard and minor drama, no. 104.

Denison, Thomas Stewart. *The sparkling cup.* Chicago: T. S. Denison, 1877.

Dunn, E. C. *Lost; a temperance drama in five acts.* Rockford, Illinois: E. C. Dunn, 1877.

Durivage, John E. *Hot Corn; Life Scene of New York.* Promptscript, 1854.

Elwyn, Lizzie May. *A ruined life; or, The curse of intemperance.* Clyde, Ohio: O. A. D. Ames, 1904. Ames' series of standard and minor drama, no. 452.

_____. *Switched off. A temperance farce.* Clyde, Ohio: O. A. D. Ames, 1899. Ames' series of standard and minor drama, no. 413.

Gilbert, Clayton H. *Rescued; an original temperance drama.* Clyde, Ohio: O. A. D. Ames, 187-. Ames' series of standard and minor drama, no. 51.

Hotchkiss, Zort P. *The Good Templars' drama of Saved, written expressly for the I[nternational] O[organization of] G[ood] T[emplars] . . . and presented in "faith, hope and charity".* Richmond, Indiana: Telegraph Steam Printing Co., 1874.

Howe, William Oscar. *The drunkard's dream; or, The spirit of 1876. A moral domestic drama, in five acts and six tableaux.* Fitchburg, Mass.: Sentinel Printing Co., 1876.

Jerrold, Douglas William. *Fifteen Years of a drunkard's life. A melodrama in three acts.* New York: Samuel French, 185-. French's standard drama, no. 347; and New York: Happy Hours Company, 185-. The Acting drama series, no. 55. note: in performance from 1830.

Johnston, Robert. *Rum; or The crusade of temperance . . . in four acts.* Philadelphia: R. Johnston, 1874.

Jones, William A. *The drunkard's home, his cruelty, his eccentricities, his reflection, his remorse, and reformation.* Self printed, 1895.

Latour, H. J. *True wealth; a temperance drama in four scenes.* New York: The National Temperance Society and Publishing House, 1889.

Linn, J. Henry. *The fatal step; or, Whiskey unmasked.* Montezuma, Indiana: J. H. Linn, 1879.

McBride, H. Elliott. *On the brink; or, The reclaimed husband. A temperance drama in two acts.* Chicago: T. S. Denison, 1878.

_____. *Reclaimed; or, Sunshine comes at last.* Philadelphia: P. Garrett & Co., 1891.

_____. *The stolen child; or, A New Hampshire man in Boston. A temperance drama in two acts.* New York: Dick & Fitzgerald, 1882; later published by Wehman Brothers, New York.

_____. *Two drams of brandy; a temperance play.* New York: O. A. Roorbach, 1881. Acting drama, no. 149.

_____. *Under the curse; a temperance drama.* New York: O. A. Roorbach, 1881. Acting drama, no. 148.

McCloskey, J. J. *The fatal glass; or, The curse of drink. A temperance drama in three acts.* Brooklyn: J. J. McCloskey, 1872.

McFall, B. G. *Among the moonshiner; or, A drunkard's legacy . . . in three acts.* Clyde, Ohio: O. A. D. Ames, 1897.

Morton, Charles H. *Three years in a man-trap; an original temperance drama . . . founded on the popular story of the same name by T. S. Arthur [1872].* Camden: New Republic Print, 1873. Prompt book.

Pratt, William W. *Ten nights in a bar-room; a drama in five acts, dramatized from T. S. Arthur's novel of the same name [1858].* New York: Samuel French, 186-. French's standard drama, no. 339.

Robinson, Solon. *Hot Corn; or, Life scenes in New York illustrated . . . [based on an editorial] by Horace Greeley.* New York: DeWitt and Davenport, 1854, as novel.

Seymour, Harry. *Aunt Dinah's pledge . . . in two acts . . . correctly printed from the prompter's copy, with the cast of characters, costumes, &c . . .* New York: Dick & Fitzgerald, 185-; and New York: Samuel French, 186-. French's standard drama, no. 357.

_____. *The temperance doctor. A moral drama in two acts . . . dramatized from the Story of the Temperance doctor.* New York: Samuel French, 187-. French's standard drama, no. 356.

Shultz, Eveline Spooner. *Twentieth century temperance socials.* New York: Hints Publishing Company, 1902.

Smith, William Henry. *The drundard; or, The fallen saved! A moral dramatic drama in five acts. Printed from the acting copy with the stage business, cast, etc.* New York: H. Long and Brother, 1847; New York: Samuel French, 185-.

Taylor, C. W. *The Drunkard's Warning; a temperance drama in three acts.* New York: Samuel French, 187-. French's standard drama, no. 355.

Taylor, Tom. *The bottle; or, Cause and effect. A drama in two acts.* New York: John Douglas, 1847; London: T. H. Lacy, 1855; New York: Samuel French, 187-.

Vautrot, George S. *At last; a temperance drama.* Clyde, Ohio: O. A. D. Ames, 1879. Ames' series of standard and minor drama, no. 73.

Whalen, E. C. *Under the spell; a temperance drama in four acts.* Chicago: T. S. Denison, 1890.

Wilkins, W. Henri. *Three glasses a day, or; The broken home*. Clyde, Ohio: O. A. D. Ames, 1878. Ames' series of standard and minor drama, no. 63.

Woodward, T. Trask. *The social glass; or, Victims of the bottle. The great sensational temperance drama in five acts*. New York and London: Samuel French, 1887.

TREASURES IN THE ATTIC:
GLEANINGS FROM THE PRIVATE ARCHIVE
OF HENRY CLAY BARNABEE

by Martha Schmoyer LoMonaco

Henry Clay Barnabee was one of America' foremost interpreters of comic or light opera, a leading popular entertainment of the late nineteenth-century. The "Dean of Light Opera," as he was known, was a household name from coast to coast, first as an individual performer and later as manager and principal artist for The Bostonians, the most successful comic opera company of its time. The Bostonians toured throughout America and Europe for twenty-five years and were credited by at least one critic as having done "more for music than any other company in the United States."[1] Yet, Barnabee and his Bostonians are virtually unknown today. They are the neglected heroes of an entertainment that realized its heyday a century ago and, except for Gilbert & Sullivan, is rarely revived.

I rediscovered Barnabee and The Bostonians in the attic of the Portsmouth, New Hampshire, Public Library where two trunks of memorabilia, painstakingly gathered by Barnabee and his wife, have lain for over half a century. In all probability, Barnabee, who was fond of his hometown of Portsmouth, left his greatest treasures in its care upon his death in 1917. Although some of his assiduously catalogued "volumes" appear to be missing, it is still obvious that Barnabee never threw away a thing in his life. Every shred of his theatrical career, from favorable and unfavorable notices to hundreds of photographs, broadsides, and playbills to the many letters from adoring fans, were neatly pasted in scrapbooks that document his nearly fifty years on the professional stage. Much of the material is devoted to

---

MARTHA SCHMOYER LOMONACO is an Assistant Professor of fine Arts and Resident Theatre Director at Fairfield University in Connecticut.

the Bostonians and warm reminiscences of individual company members.

Barnabee was an established entertainer of some repute long before The Bostonians troupe was conceived. The theatre, however, did not immediately beckon him to a full-time career. While earning his living as a dry-goods clerk, Barnabee performed in amateur theatricals, mostly under the auspices of the Mercantile Library of Boston. He also lent his splendid bass voice to various church choirs, notably the well-known quartet of the Unitarian Church at Jamaica Plain, Massachusetts. It was not until 1865, when a growing reputation in and around Boston as a performer of comic songs and sketches, convinced him to devote his talents exclusively to the stage: "Being able to sing a serious song as well as a comic one, take part in a duo, trio or quartet, speak a piece, and tell a story, I was considered, even at the advanced price, the cheapest and most economical bargain-package 'on the cirkit.' "[2]

Barnabee dates his first "actual histrionic appearance on a real stage" as November 9, 1866 at a benefit for R. F. McClannin at the Boston Museum.[3] He played Toby Twinkle in *All That Glitters Is Not Gold*, sang "Simon the Cellarer," a favorite in his repertoire of comic songs, and played Cox to William Warren's Box in the famous afterpiece by Madison Morton. Sometime the following year, he introduced a comic piece that became synonymous with the name Barnabee: "Of the songs, the one with which my name is somewhat identified, and which I have been afraid, but it might form a portion of my epitaph, will readily occur to you as having the most effect upon an audience, I mean of course 'The Cork Leg.' "[4] The immense popularity of this song and its importance in establishing his career cannot be underestimated, although one journalist, writing in 1896, did carry the legend a bit far:

> Barnabee first sang 'The Cork Leg' on his twenty-first birthday. Before the year was over, he sang it an average of more than three times a day, or about 1100 times a year. He has never missed singing it a single day since. So for 40 years he has sung 'The Cork Leg' 1100 times a year, singing it in all sorts of places, under all imaginary conditions and before every kind of people.[5]

If the writer's numbers were exaggerated, the widespread fame of the piece was not. The fact that Barnabee performed this physically and vocally strenuous song well into his seventies, attests to the public's demand for what readily became an old-time favorite.

In 1870, Barnabee formed the first of numerous concert companies which toured the United States, largely through lyceum engagements, for the next nine years and established his reputation nationally. In an 1878 biographical sketch, it is evident that Barnabee had already solidified the professional qualities that would be cited throughout his career:

> There is no American musical artist of the present day who has contributed as largely to the entertainment of his fellow-man. . . . Gifted by nature with a noble bass voice, and with a keen sense of the comic side of human nature, he happily blends artistic nicety with humorous expression, so that his public performances always recommend themselves not only to the lovers of fun, but as well to those who can appreciate the finer touches of art, and who are disposed to measure the capabilities of a singer by something more than the mere power to create a laugh. . . . He is, so far as his humorous efforts go, a true musical comedian, in the same sense that such actors as Warren and Jefferson are comedians, his artistic qualities lifting him far above the level of the buffoon and 'comique.'[6]

The biographer goes on to emphasize Barnabee's predilection for "good clean fun," which is especially noteworthy in an era when popular tastes in entertainment were inclined towards the lavish and lascivious:

> There is one noticeable characteristic of all the efforts of Mr. Barnabee which deserves mention on account of the prevalent tendency of both professional and amateur performers. His songs and sketches are irresistibly comical, but they never hint at anything but the purest fun. The temptation to provoke a laugh at the expense of good taste is never yielded to by Mr. Barnabee, and the high standard so successfully maintained by him for years proves that coarseness is not necessarily a part of the outfit of public entertainment.[7]

The year 1879 marked a turning point in Barnabee's career with the founding of the light opera company that would dominate the American musical stage for the next twenty-five years. The Boston Ideal Opera Company, which would form the nucleus of The Bostonians, was conceived by the manager of the Boston Theatre who wanted to do a musically worthy production of Gilbert and Sullivan's *H.M.S. Pinafore*. He sought the help of Miss E. H. Ober of the Roberts Lyceum Bureau to assemble the "ideal" cast (hence, the name) for his production. *Pinafore* premiered April 14, 1879 and became an instantaneous success, giving Barnabee one of his most memorable roles as Sir Joseph Porter. The Ideals rapidly produced an equally successful encore with Franz von Suppe's *Fatinitza* which opened a scant ten weeks later. The company flourished between 1879 and 1887 and presented a total of twenty-two different operas by Barnabee's count.

Problems began for the Ideals in 1885 when Mr. W. H. Foster took over as company manager. He transformed the company from a tight ensemble of seasoned professionals to a star-studded vehicle for particular young prima donnas. After two mediocre seasons, Barnabee, along with Tom Karl and William MacDonald, decided to form their own company which was christened The Bostonians in order to "keep up our connection with the glorious past."[8] During the spring of 1887, the press eagerly reported on this famous break-up. In one interview, Barnabee explained their decision:

> We propose to have an operatic organization with no stars, but one in which all the leading people shall be competent and clever. The people, I believe, enjoyed our old-time performance because the ensemble was superior and the work in general well done. Our efforts the "Mascot," "Patience," and other light operas pleased the public for the reason that there was no gap created in the performance when any one of the leading characters left the stage.[9]

The Bostonians had no trouble picking up where The Ideals left off and, according to Barnabee, "had the satisfaction of being everywhere hailed as the real survivors and heirs of the late lamented Ideals."[10] They opened with a revival of *Fatinitza* and a new offering, Offenbach's *The Poachers* which provided two solid hits for their first season in 1888. The company included many of the old Ideals which, in addition to the three founder/managers, featured Marie Stone (Mrs. MacDonald), George Frothingham and Agnes Huntington. Personnel changed frequently during its sixteen years of existence (twenty-five counting the nine Ideal years), but early on the company acquired its most famous prima donna, Jessie Bartlett Davis, and other audience favorites including Eugene Cowles, Edwin W. Hoff and Josephine Bartlett. Many felt that it was this nucleus of talented performers working together over many years that gave The Bostonians its unique identity:

> Critics and ticket buyers recognized that their voices were excellent enough, that the costumes and setting were well enough executed and the casting was competent, but these things might have been said of a number of troupes. Above these were the special virtues. There was in the first place no individual star, there were at least six principals of equal competence. They were largely from Boston and grew into a singular attachment one

with the other. There was geniality and richness in their private lives and this seemed to color their work.[11]

The Bostonians garnered honors and laudatory notices wherever they went. "To say that it was given by The Bostonians is to say that it was well done" was the prevalent critical and popular reaction even if the quality of the opera itself, such as Herbert's *Prince Ananias*, was doubtful.[12] Critics frequently cited the company's untainted respectability, fine sense of ensemble with a noted absence of individual stars, consistently high vocal quality, strong patriotism, and dedication to cultivating and producing new American operas as its special strengths. The most enduring aspect, however, and one that was influenced by Barnabee himself, was The Bostonians' pledge to provide clean-cut entertainment. As one commentator lamented upon the company's demise in 1904:

> For unquestionably, Mr. Barnabee and his associates stood for the higher ideals in comic opera. When the stage was given over to empty and vulgar 'shows' in which the staple was the profuse and immodest display of feminine charms, The Bostonians held firmly to the older and better traditions. They did their best to raise the public taste, and offered the best light operas they could get.[13]

The Bostonians did have their share of mixed and unfavorable reviews. An early one, quoted here, considers what may have been an inherent flaw in Barnabee's ideal company:

> The Bostonians are one of those companies which, like certain people, make one wonder why they are not more attractive. . . . They are not bores at all, but at the same time they are not extravagantly entertaining. They never slight their work, yet there is an indefinable something – a spirit of vivacity, an individual interest, a tempered enthusiasm – wanting in them. . . . Not one of them is in any way distinguished – save Mr. MacDonald for height and Miss Corden for length of hair. And by "distinguished" one does not mean marked by absolute genius, but simply distinguished from an average mass by a spice, a flavor, a soupcon of something which everybody else has not got.[14]

The critic goes on to suggest that the very qualities Barnabee and company sought to enhance might ultimately work against them:

> They are an exceedingly good company, much better than the average, but they are without personal fascination. They lack daring, audacity, and are tamely cautious in everything they do. . . . Watching them – a collection of average good artists, all on a

par–one is worked upon to wonder whether a company conducted on the star system is better or worse. We have all inveighed against the star system and clamored for a change. In The Bostonians we have a distinct change–nobody is a star and nobody is absolutely poor–yet is it a change very much for the better?[15]

The troupe of "average good artists–all on a par" was soon to discover that its system worked only so long as it produced excellent material; mediocre or poor works required the mystique and charisma that only stellar performers could provide. Soon after this article appeared, The Bostonians premiered what, ironically, would be both its greatest success and the catalyst to its downfall. Smith and DeKoven's *Robin Hood*, offered during the 1890–91 season, catapulted the company to its height of popularity and gave Barnabee his finest role as the Sheriff of Nottingham. Although *Robin Hood* became the mainstay of The Bostonians' repertoire, it never had an adequate successor. As many critics noted, a company cannot go on forever with only one great opera and the troupe, despite heroic efforts, simply could not find one. Every subsequent offering was compared to *Robin Hood* and inevitably was declared inferior. It was not until the 1896–97 season that the company found a second if lesser hit in Herbert and Smith's *The Serenade*. According to Barnabee, this success allowed them "five more fat years with the repertoire thus strengthened."[16]

Of the nineteen new operas The Bostonians premiered in sixteen years, only these two could be considered successful. With Barnabee at the helm, the company managed to struggle on until 1904 when a "Gala 25th Birthday Party," celebrated at New York's Academy of Music with Joseph Jefferson presiding, inaugurated their farewell tour. Sadly, The Bostonians failed to go out in a blaze of glory; rather, the company died miserably in Atlantic City, New Jersey, with a final offering ironically entitled *The Queen of Laughter*.

The principal reasons for The Bostonians' demise have already been offered, but there were other problems. Undoubtedly, the company's commitment to presenting only new American operas, although a noble undertaking, hurt them far more than it helped. As Barnabee lamented after three successive failures: "Our lesson was to be slowly and painfully learned, that if the American public really discriminated in favor of home-made art, which was doubtful, they were not going to rave over it in its new-fangled light opera habiliments."[17] Also, the prudish conventionality of the troupe finally served to defeat it, especially with the popular surge of burlesque and other coarse entertainments. One critic put it this way:

The Bostonians, I honestly believe, are under the evil spell of their name, and . . . they are trying to live up to it. All their stifling of frolicsome humor; their serenity of expression, and that atmosphere of intellectual propriety which surrounds them, comes from this attempt. If they had a less baleful title they would be a happier people. So, I am sure, would their audiences.[18]

Although this appraisal was made at the beginning of their career, it proved to be prophetic. The truth is that by 1904, public taste had changed but The Bostonians did not change accordingly. Barnabee regretted not having retired the troupe sooner, while the tide was obviously turning. Unfortunately, instead of ending their career with a respectable bow, The Bostonians became unpopular remnants of a former age.

Despite the volatile artistic tastes of the American public at the turn-of-the century, the collapse of The Bostonians was a profound loss to the entertainment world. America has always championed an unsophisticated, unabashedly simple and homespun form of native entertainment which, undoubtedly, was at the heart of The Bostonians' appeal. In an age when America was still discovering its own artistic voice, The Bostonians were proud contributors to that quest. That the troupe was consistently popular for so long a time, however, made the company notable among American performers. "They took hold upon the country as no other organization ever did," one critic contended, adding, "it is apparent that they were the ideal troupe in the ideal show for the years in which they played."[19] Another critic, writing immediately after The Bostonians' break-up, captured what was probably the essence of their success: "The controlling spirits were men of business ability, tact, and with a personal knowledge of the public taste and its musical desires. They catered to that taste and filled that desire in an eminently satisfactory manner for a quarter of a century, and nothing but regret can be felt at the circumstance of their retirement."[20]

The end of The Bostonians did not, by any means, mark the end of Barnabee as well. He immediately embarked on what would have proven a lucrative vaudeville tour when, in the second week of performances, he suffered a severe knee injury that terminated his engagement. Although he gained only partial recovery of his leg, he still continued to perform whenever possible. It is fair to surmise that Barnabee, like many entertainers, needed the constant devotion of his public. In a 1910 letter to his friend Fred Chapman, Barnabee discussed a recent performance in Syracuse where there was "a most brilliant audience that cheered and laughed itself hoarse over our efforts. It is worth living for." In the same letter, Barnabee enclosed a clipping from *The Boston Globe* commemorating his seventy-seventh birthday that proclaimed him to be "well preserved" and a "wit as keen as ever."[21] Much the same sentiment, he declared to Chapman, was expressed by his ever admiring public:

> I am in frequent receipt of the most flattering tributes of love, affection, and admiration from all parts of my beloved country, from friends, stranger friends, and the multitude who meet me on the street, in Boston, whenever I go in to the city and almost throw their arms around me, and looking *just the same*, they all declare, as I did half a century ago.[22]

In 1906, Barnabee received two testimonial benefits in his honor, one in New York and one in Boston. An account appearing in the *New York Herald* of the Lambs' Club tribute at the Broadway Theatre, December 11, 1906, attests to the stature he attained among his theatre colleagues:

> It would take much space to tell all about the performance. Those who took part included practically all of the stars, leading men and women, and many others of the stage celebrities now appearing in Broadway. Mr. Victor Herbert and his orchestra played a fantasie from 'The Serenade' as an overture, which was followed by an address by Mrs. Fiske and written by Mr. Clay M. Greene, which paid a tribute to Mr. Barnabee.
>
> Others on the program, which began at one o'clock and lasted until after six o'clock, included Mr. Lew Fields and company, in the duel scene from 'About Town'; Miss Blanche Ring, in some songs; Mr. Henry Miller and Miss Margaret Anglin, in the first act of 'The Great Divide'; Miss May Irwin, in a song; Miss Eleanor Robson and company, in a one-act play entitled 'A Tenement Tragedy,' and Miss Rose Stahl and company, in second act of 'The Chorus Lady'; Miss Lillian Russell, accompanied by her daughter, Miss Dorothy, at the piano in two songs; Miss Hattie Williams, in a selection from 'The Little Cherub,' supported by a chorus made up of well-known actors, including Messrs. Fritz Williams, Edmund Breese, Ernest Lambart, Edward Holland and W.L. Abingdon; Miss Louise Dresser in a song entitled 'My Gal Sal'; Mr. William Gillette, Miss Marie Doro and Miss Lucille La Verne, in the supper scene from 'Clarice,' and Mr. Henry Clay Barnabee and all of the principal comedians now appearing in Broadway in the tinkers' chorus from 'Robin Hood.'
>
> Others who helped to make the benefit the big success it was

were Messrs. John Drew, Cyrle Bellew, Forbes Robertson, Henry
Leoni, Miss Anna Held and Mlle. Dazie.[23]

The Boston benefit, although deficient in as many nationally known
luminaries, was no less complementary to Barnabee, as *The Boston
Globe* relates: "Surely no man in the profession in Boston ever got a
more convincing testimony than Mr. Barnabee of the regard in which
he was held."[24]

"That prince of comedians and the Joe Jefferson of the comic opera
stage" died in Boston 16 December 1917 at the age of eighty-four.[25]
His memory, however, presumably died with those people who
recalled his unique brand of humor and song. Although recent history
has forgotten him, a book heralding noted actors of the day published
in 1901, did not:

> Few names have been more familiar to the amusement of the
> public of the United States during the present generation than
> that of Henry Clay Barnabee, who as a singer, impersonator, and
> operatic artist has maintained a position and pursued a career
> which have reflected credit upon the annals of the musical and
> dramatic stage of this country.[26]

ENDNOTES:

[1]Clipping, *Cambell's Illustrated Monthly*, n.d., Henry Clay Barnabee Collection, Special Collections, Portsmouth Public Library, Portsmouth, New
Hampshire (hereafter cited as Barnabee Collection).

[2]*Reminiscences of Henry Clay Barnabee, Being an Attempt to Account for His
Life, with Some Excuses for His Professional Career*, ed. George Leon
Varney (Boston: Chapple Publishing Co., 1913), 155.

[3]*Barnabee*, 175.

[4]Barnabee to C. E. L. Wingate, 14 June 1887, Harvard Theatre Collection,
Harvard University, Cambridge, Massachusetts (hereafter cited as
Harvard Theatre Collection).

[5]Clipping, *Saturday Evening Herald*, 20 October 1896, Barnabee Collection.

[6]"Biographical Sketch of a Popular Musical Artist and Humorist," *The Boston
Times*, 23 June 1878, Barnabee Collection.

[7]Ibid.

[8]*Barnabee*, 364.

[9]Clipping, Detroit, Michigan daily newspaper, 4 March 1887, Barnabee
Collection.

[10]*Barnabee*, 366.

[11]Clipping, "As The Bostonians Caroled A Half Century Ago," *Boston Evening Transcript*, 27 December 1930, Harvard Theatre Collection.

[12]Clipping, *Boston Herald*, 28 February 1895, Barnabee Collection.

[13]Clipping, "The Bostonians – A Shock Caused by their Disbandment," 1904,
Harvard Theatre Collection.

14Clipping, *The Argonaut*, San Francisco, CA, 21 April 1890, Barnabee Collection.

15Ibid.

16*Barnbee*, 420.

17*Barnabee*, 402.

18Clipping, *The Stage*, 21 December 1889, Barnabee Collection.

19"As The Bostonians Caroled a Half Century Ago," *Boston Evening Transcript*, 27 December 1930, Harvard Theatre Collection.

20Clipping, "Early Triumphs of the Famous Bostonians," *Boston Sunday Globe*, 30 October 1904, Barnabee Collection.

21Barnabee to Fred Chapman, 10 December 1910, Harvard Theatre Collection.

22Ibid.

23*Barnabee*, 429.

24*Barnabee*, 431.

25Clipping, *The Progress*, 4 May 1895, Barnabee Collection.

26A. D. Storms, ed., *The Players Blue Book* (Worcester, Massachusetts: Sutherland and Storms, 1901), 88.

"THE MYSTERY OF THE SOUTH END": THE BOSTON CYCLORAMA OF THE BATTLE OF GETTYSBURG

by X. Theodore Barber

In 1885 a Boston newspaper declared that "there is nothing in Boston better worth seeing" than the Cyclorama of the Battle of Gettysburg.[1] A type of panorama, this immensely popular attraction created by Paul D. Philippoteaux was on display in a specially constructed building on Termont Street. Although hundreds of panoramas were on exhibition throughout Europe and North America during their heyday in the nineteenth century, only a small number have survived, including this particular work which is now permanently located at Gettysburg National Park, Pennsylvania.[2] It is especially fortunate that the building which originally housed this cyclorama also still remains and is probably the only example of its kind in the United States.

The panorama is one of a number of popular entertainments, like the magic lantern, peep show, and diorama, which fall into the category of optical and mechanical amusements. These entertained audiences by means of visual imagery and special effects and were, so to speak, a kind of "actorless theatre," even though they were often accompanied by a live performer in the form of a lecturer or narrator. Patented in 1787 by Edinburgh portrait painter Robert Barker, the panorama was a huge painting done on a cylindrical canvas which surrounded the audience with a 360 degree view. A special building was required for its presentation, and Barker's 1794 rotunda erected in London generally set the pattern for later buildings of this type. He hung his panorama around the circumference of the building,

---

X. THEODORE BARBER has studied film and theatre history at Harvard University and New York University. His articles have appeared in such journals as *Film History, The Drama Review,* and *Theatre Studies.*

which measured 90 feet in diameter, in such a way that the spectators felt themselves to be standing in the midst of some huge vista that had no clear boundaries.

Barker's invention proved popular and quickly spread throughout Europe. Depicting events and places in the news, panoramas served as illustrators of significant occurrences in the decades before the introduction of pictures in newspapers. Large-scale spectacular events were, of course, common themes given the grandiose dimensions of most panoramas, and not surprisingly, the paintings were frequently celebrations of nationalism. Battle scenes which emphasized a particular country's triumphant and heroic actions were typical. Napoleon himself commissioned seven panoramas to be displayed in Paris to glorify his exploits, although his ultimate defeat prevented their completion. Some panoramas merely depicted landscapes or cities, but even these had nationalistic tendencies. A view of Salzburg, for example, was a source of national pride to Austria.

The panorama was introduced to the United States in 1795 when a copy of Barker's view of London was put on display in New York. In 1818, John Vanderlyn erected the first permanent panorama building in America. Located opposite City Hall in New York, it housed Vanderlyn's painting of Versailles. This panorama was not successful, since Americans, it seemed, would rather forget their European past and instead admire their own cultural accomplishments. As Vanderlyn wrote, "Had I bestowed my time and attention in painting a view of New York instead of Versailles I should, I am now convinced, have reaped more profits."[3] Despite this problem, Vanderlyn's panorama happens to survive and can be seen at the Metropolitan Museum of Art, New York.

In general, the first panoramas did not reach wide audiences in America because they could not tour the country efficiently. Not only was the transportation system poor, but structures which could hold these huge canvases were hard to come by. In the 1820's Americans developed a new type of panorama which did not need a rotunda to be shown. The moving panorama, as it was called, was a very long painting which was rolled from one upright spool onto another, so that the scenes on it passed in front of the spectators. The subjects of these panoramas were usually landscapes as seen from moving vehicles.

By the late 1830's a new word "cyclorama" was coined to differentiate the 360 degree paintings from the moving panoramas. But as the nineteenth century progressed, cycloramas developed some unique characteristics. For one thing, they became much larger than the earlier panoramas and measured sometimes upwards of 150 feet in diameter. For another, they began to include cut-outs and actual objects positioned directly in front of the painting itself, so as to blend with it and create a three-dimensional effect. Frenchman Jean-Charles Langlois was famous for developing this foreground effect, but it was two other French artists, Henri F. Philippoteaux and his son Paul, who refined it further and helped to revive the panorama in the final decades of the nineteenth century, a time when its popularity was on the decline because of the general availability of photographs, newspaper illustrations, and engravings of important events. None of these could match the excitement of being transported to the seemingly real, three-dimensional environment of the Philippoteaux cycloramas.

An established painter of battle scenes, Henri Philippoteaux, born in 1815, turned to creating cycloramas late in his life. Son Paul, born in 1846, began receiving instructions in art from his father at the age of ten. At sixteen he studied under Cabanel and then went on to receive high honors at the École des Beaux Arts. Americans first became acquainted with the cycloramas of the Philippoteauxs (father and son) when Colonel Fortuné Liénard's copy of their *Siege of Paris* toured the United States in 1875 and the years immediately thereafter. This work inspired several Chicago entrepreneurs to commission the Philippoteauxs to create the first cyclorama ever to depict the Battle of Gettysburg.

Memories of the Civil War were still alive in the late 1800's. Veterans were eager to recall their battle experiences, and other wanted actually to see what they had heard about. Even though the war had, at first, served to divide the country, it produced a number of heroes who could be admired by both sides and it helped to define the character of the nation as a whole.

In order to prepare for painting a cyclorama of Gettysburg, Paul Philippoteaux came to America around 1880 and spent several months on the battlefield making sketches of the countryside. He also hired a local photographer to take three series of pictures, each series focusing on a different region of the landscape—foreground, middleground, and background. In addition, Philippoteaux consulted the maps on file in the War Department in Washington and interviewed Generals Hancock, Doubleday, and others. All this was done to achieve as much authenticity as possible.

Paul Philippoteaux painted the cyclorama in Brussels in 1882–1883. Although Henri had had a hand in its creation, he was to die soon after its completion. Displayed for a short time in Belgium, the cyclorama was brought to Chicago where it opened on October 22, 1883. Supposedly half a million people visited it the first year, and this popularity inspired C. L. Willoughby, a Chicago merchant, to contract with Philippoteaux to create a second version of his painting to be shown in Boston.

The Boston Cyclorama of the Battle of Gettysburg, measuring 400 feet in circumference and 50 in height, was executed in a revolving circular studio in Paris. The canvas was made of flax soaked in linseed oil. The paints used were oils, tinsel being added occasionally in the depiction of bayonets or bursting bombshells. By means of a grid system, Philippoteaux and his assistants transferred the series of sketches and photographs which had been made at Gettysburg onto the canvas. Each artist, at his position on a set of scaffolds, was responsible for painting his specialty—be it faces, uniforms or horses.

Finished in 1884, the cyclorama was shipped to Boston wrapped on a huge steel roller. When it arrived, the roller was set up vertically on a scaffold which moved on tracks around the circumference of the rotunda. The painting was then unrolled and mounted. Wooden flooring was installed in front of the picture in such a way as to imitate the rise and fall of the Gettysburg landscape. Soil and grass were laid down, and trees, wheat, stone fences, cannons and all manner of military paraphernalia were carefully added to the foreground area in order to blend with the objects in the painting. Some of the effects were especially ingenious. For instance, a well which began as a three-dimensional structure in the foreground was continued into the painting, so that some of its stones were real and others were but representations on canvas.[4]

After the cyclorama was set up, Philippoteaux, who had come to Boston, invited various generals to visit it. Using their suggestions, he made further revisions in the painting in order to improve its accuracy.[5] Changes were also made in labelling particular figures in the cyclorama as new information about battle positions came to light. For example, the general who was named as Alex Hays in the first diagram sold as a key to the painting became John Gibbons in a revised diagram.

Charles A. Cummings and Willard T. Sears, a prominent Boston architects, designed the Cyclorama Building at 541 Tremont Street in the South End. It was 138 feet in diameter and 50 ½ feet high to the eaves. The dome, made of tin with a glass skylight, was 75 feet from the ground at its highest point. The structure was distinguished for being the first steel frame building in Boston and for having one of the largest domes in the country.[6]

Standing as a colossal monument to past glories, the building itself reflected national pride. A sense of militarism was also conveyed by the exterior architecture done in a Victorian feudal style, complete with two guard towers, turreted walls, and battlements. The facade, however, had little to do with the Gettysburg subject matter of the cyclorama. The purpose of the feudal design was to arouse people's curiosity and thus drum up business. A handbill advertised the cyclo-rama as "The Mystery of the South End," and one newspaper reported that until the doors opened to the press on December 20, 1884, people were "mystified" as to how "a strange fortress-looking building was to be put to use when finished."7

Open everyday except Sunday, the hours were 9 am to 11 pm. Admission was 50 cents for adults and 25 for children. The public entered through the central arched door and found a furnished parlor inside the larger tower on the left and a ticket office in the tower on the right. After descending a short flight of stairs and depositing a ticket in the receptacle guarded by a doorkeeper in military uniform, spectators walked along a lengthy, dimly lit corridor to a winding flight of steps which led to the center of the viewing platform.

As in Robert Barker's panorama building, viewers stood on an ele-vated, circular stage in the center of the auditorium. This stage kept people at an even distance from the painting and represented some high vantage point which provided a good view of the landscape. The platform for the Gettysburg cyclorama could hold 900 people and represented Cemetery Ridge, a raised spot in the thick of the battle.

A canopy suspended above the auditorium was painted to repre-sent the sky, and it served the same function as the one in Barker's building – to hide both the upper edge of the painting and the source of light. Besides the skylight, there were a number of electric lights hung from the dome. These bulbs lit the cyclorama at night and during bad weather. Although natural light was preferred for its real-istic effect, it was a perpetual source of difficulty for exhibitions of this kind because it was often unreliable or unequally distributed.

The overall lighting design, however, was cleverly arranged, according to Barker's principles. Spectators became accustomed to the dark as they walked down the dimly lit corridor. Then on reaching the top of the platform, they were dazzled by the contrast between the darkness and the colorful painting which seemed brilliantly illu-minated. With nothing lit but the cyclorama itself, they lost their sense of orientation and could not judge their distance from it or its painted horizon. In addition, since the light came from above, specta-tors cast no shadows on the painting – something which could poten-tially spoil the illusion of reality.

The viewers were supposed to be standing just inside Hancock's lines on the afternoon of July 3, 1863, the third day of battle. At west could be seen Pickett's charge on the Union position. In the east, Federal re-enforcements were hurrying to the center from Culp's Hill and Little Round Top, while General Hunt surveyed the scene through field glasses. General Hancock's position was in the south and behind him was the irregular line of battle stretching towards Round Top. The field hospital was located in the north.

Opera glasses were available to the public to help in viewing the picture and to enhance the illusory conception that the images were very distant. A fact-filled programme book was sold, and on certain days, Major Bancroft, a local veteran, gave talks on the battle and pointed out prominent features in the painting. The viewing experience was meant to be educational. Not only did the cyclorama entertain, but it also provided information about the history of the war and its place in the making of the country.

Even though the cyclorama was promoted as being highly educational and accurate, it actually had some unrealistic or unauthentic aspects. The events depicted in the painting did not in reality happen simultaneously, but rather over the course of an entire afternoon, and the artist, in trying to make his work as exciting as possible, was very selective in his choice of subjects. Furthermore, Philippoteaux's early training in Romantic art influenced the style of the Gettysburg canvas which was posed and melodramatic, full of emotion, color and heroic action. Blood and gore, however, were downplayed, since the artist did not wish to offend or disgust his audience.[8]

In all, the cyclorama took the harsh realities of war and rendered them thrilling and palatable to general audiences. A good twenty years had elapsed since the battle had taken place, and people were ready and able to forget its more painful aspects. Since the nation was now unified and at peace, audiences, as the reviewers noted, could feel nothing but patriotism when gazing at the painting. It served as a testament to the country's present prosperity rather than former difficulties. The appeal of the work even led Philippoteaux to create additional cyclorama of Gettysburg—one for New York and another for Philadelphia.

As for the Boston painting, it finally ended its run in 1889 and was rolled up and stored. Abused and forgotten for many years, it was purchased in 1942 by the National Park Service which restored it in 1960 for display at Gettysburg. Some sections of the canvas are missing, however, and in its present state, the painting is smaller than it was originally.

The Boston rotunda continued to present other cycloramas for a short while after the removal of the Philippoteaux work, but the structure then became a sports arena and automobile garage, amongst other things, before settling on its present function as headquarters of the Boston Center for the Arts.[9] Although portions of the building have been remodelled, some of its original turrets, battlements, and mock windows are still there today. In seeing both the original painting and the building which housed it, we can acquire a sense of the spectacular nature of this nineteenth century entertainment which inspired many a visitor.

Particularly valuable primary sources on the Gettysburg cycloramas of Philippoteaux are the programmes that accompanied these paintings. Usually included in each programme was background material regarding the creation of the cyclorama, a diagram of the painting that identified the action and figures represented in it, and excerpts of laudatory newspaper reviews. Extant examples of these programmes can be found in some major repositories including the Chicago Historical Society, Boston Public Library, New York Public Library, and Virginia State Library. Also useful are the vintage photographs of the Gettysburg cycloramas, sets of which were often sold as souvenirs. Such institutions as the Boston Public Library, Boston Center for the Arts, and Historical Society of Pennsylvania have examples. For more detailed information on the exhibition history of the cycloramas, newspapers have to be searched. The Boston Public Library's microfilm holdings of newspapers proved especially useful in researching this article.

An historical overview of the Boston Cyclorama Building is provided by unpublished reports held by the Boston Landmarks Commission. Dick Card of Boston's South End Historical Society was generous in sharing sources and his own research on the history of the Boston structure. Furthermore, the files of the Gettysburg National Military Park have material on the Gettysburg cyclorama painting originally displayed in Boston, including its later history and restoration.

ENDNOTES

[1]*Boston Watchman* 19 February 1885.

[2]For a list of extant panoramas, see Evelyn J. Fruitema and Paul A. Zoetmulder, eds., *The Panorama Phenomenon: Mesdag Panorama 1881-1981* (The Hague: Foundation for the Preservation of the Centenarian Mesdag Panorama, 1981) 112-13.

[3]John Vanderlyn, letter, 1824, quoted in The Metropolitan Museum of Art, *The Panoramic View of the Palace and Gardens of Versailles, Painted by John Vanderlyn* (New York: The Metropolitan Museum of Art, 1956).

[4]For information on the painting, installation, and display of Philippoteaux's Gettysburg cycloramas, see "The Cyclorama," *Scientific American* 6 November 1886: 296, and *Cyclorama of the Battle of Gettysburg by Paul Philippoteaux* (Boston, 1885, 1886, 1889).

[5]"The Gettysburg Cyclorama," *Boston Evening Transcript* 3 July 1913, 11.

[6]Jack Nackey, "The Origin and History of the Building Now Occupied by the Boston Flower Exchange; Formerly the Site of the Gettysburg Mural,

Called Cyclorama," unpublished report, Boston Landmarks Commission, Boston, 1–2.

[7]*Boston Sunday Herald* 21 December 1884.

[8]The *Boston Daily Transcript* 30 December 1884, discusses the painting's depiction of violence.

[9]For the later history of the Boston cyclorama painting and its rotunda, see Nackey 7–8; Rudolph Elie, "The Lost Is Found, Safe and Sound," *Boston Herald* 2 December 1952; Mary Van Meter, "The Cyclorama Building and Its Neighbors: An Area Survey of the Boston Center for the Arts. Prepared for the Massachusetts Historical Commission, 1972," unpublished report, Boston Landmarks Commission, Boston, 24–29.

THE MISSING WILL AND GEORGE M. COHAN'S "MONEY TO BURN"

by Stephen M. Vallillo

One of the main tenets of popular entertainments is that the style and personality of the performer are usually more important than the originality of the material that is performed. Performers often "borrowed" material from others. A number of vaudeville performers attracted repeat audiences year after year using the same act. Frequently performers took the same basic plot and recycled it in slightly varied forms. All these different examples show that the performer's style is more important than "literary" originality.

The handwritten manuscript of George M. Cohan's sketch "Money to Burn," that exists at the Museum of the City of New York's Theatre Collection illustrates this last idea.[1] In this sketch, first performed in 1897, Cohan recycles a plot device – the missing will – that his father Jerry Cohan had used in a short play, a device that he would again use in 1905 as the plot of *Forty-Five Minutes to Broadway*, one of his most successful musical comedies.

The handwritten manuscript of "Money to Burn" is important not only because it is the only extant vaudeville sketch performed by the Four Cohans that I am aware of, but also because it provides an informative glimpse into his approach towards theatre. This sketch, based on an idea with which Cohan was very familiar, shows that he was interested less in original plot ideas than in his own distinctive way of bringing those ideas to the stage. It also demonstrates Cohan's fledgling dramatic technique. Vaudeville sketch writing was important training for Cohan. He learned to turn a story into a play, he sharpened his use of humor, and he developed a personal style that

---

STEPHEN M. VALLILLO earned a doctorate in Performance Studies from New York University with his dissertation on Cohan as a director. He is the co-editor of *The Directory of Stage Directors*.

remained in his later work: a varied mix of comedy, songs and dance which moved quickly. As he began writing three-act musicals for Broadway, however, he grew to dislike the one-act format. "Every good vaudeville sketch is an awful waste of ideas. You give up everything you've got in that fifteen minute act."[2] His recycling of "Money to Burn" into *Forty-Five Minutes from Broadway* is a perfect illustration of this attitude.

Although he started publishing songs around 1893 and sold comic material to other performers in the mid 1890's, George M. Cohan did not write for his family's act, The Four Cohans, until November 1896 when he revised his father's sketch "Goggle's Doll House," into "Goggle's Wife" (later called "The Professor's Wife"). The twenty-minute sketch combined singing, dancing and comedy and was well received.[3] In his first sketch for his family, Cohan was already balancing what would become the three main elements of his musical comedies.

In March of 1897, the Four Cohans added another of his sketches to their repertoire. This new script, like "Goggle's Wife," derived from an earlier Jerry Cohan script.[4] "Money to Burn," a sentimental comedy with music about Susan Sweetapple, housekeeper to a rich man who died without leaving a will, was based on "A Noble Sacrifice," a two-character sketch in Jerry Cohan's own manuscript sketchbook (in the Harvard Theatre collection), about Susan Sweetapple, left unrewarded because of a missing will, and Bob Ticket, who inherits his uncle's fortune.[5] Cohan later expanded the same basic plot into *Forty-Five Minutes from Broadway*. However, the amusing characters which Cohan developed in his two versions, his songs and dances, his humor, and the tempo and style of his productions kept the unoriginal plots interesting and gave each retelling its own distinctive flavor. George M. Cohan's two versions of the missing will story are not simple remakes; instead he changed the basic story greatly in each production to meet the needs of different forms of entertainment.

Each version of the missing will story is tailored to the requirements of a specific popular entertainment form. "A Noble Sacrifice," written by Jerry Cohan for his wife Nellie and himself, was a two-person variety sketch. "Money to Burn" used all four members of the Cohan family in a musical vaudeville sketch, and *Forty-Five Minutes from Broadway* was a three-act Broadway musical comedy.

In "A Noble Sacrifice," Mrs. Cohan played Susan Sweetapple, a maid. The sketch begins after her employer's death. Susan laments the lack of a will that would leave her his estate as the entire community had expected. Mr. Pugwash, an offstage suitor, sends a letter in which he abandons her when he sees that she has not inherited the estate. Instead, Bob Ticket, the dissolute nephew, has been named the heir in the absence of a will. When he arrives, he asks Susan for food, drinks and a billiards table and announces that he has invited a young lady to see him. Susan asks to leave, and begins packing. She requests that Bob examine her trunk so he will not accuse her of taking anything that is not hers. He discovers the missing will wrapped in a calico dress his uncle had given Susan. After a short battle with his conscience, he gives her the will, leaving himself penniless. She gloats over her new-found wealth, and hires the now-destitute Bob as her servant, forcing him to serve (offstage) the young lady he had invited over. She then gets another letter from her former suitor Pugwash, declaring his affection for her. Tired of being loved only for her wealth, Susan tears up the will. Having learned humility from his servitude, Bob declares his love for Susan and they decide to marry and live happily together.

This sentimental sketch gave both Cohans a chance to perform comic bits as well as dramatic moments and pleased the audience with its happy ending. The two-person playlet fit well on a variety bill, whether in one of several touring companies that Jerry Cohan organized or on other vaudeville bills.

In 1897, when George M. Cohan wrote "Money to Burn," the Cohan family had been performing as a four-person team in vaudeville theatres across the country. In addition to Jerry and Nellie's talents and personalities, the family was well-known for George's eccentric dancing and his sister Josie's graceful skirt dancing, and "Money to Burn," which premiered in Los Angeles on March 8, 1897 utilized those talents.[6] As *The Dramatic Mirror* noted, "The elder Cohans had control of the plot while the younger members were resting between dances . . ."[7]

"Money to Burn," like Jerry Cohan's sketch, features a character named Susan Sweetapple (played by Nellie Cohan), housekeeper to a rich man who died without leaving a will. The cast also includes Liz (played by Josie), a friend of Susan; Splinters (George M.), a comic errand boy; Alphonso Jolliett (Jerry), the rakish nephew; and Carrie De Banner (Josie again), Jolliett's actress friend. Although the handwritten manuscript for the sketch does not include the first page and any pages following page thirty, it does present a good picture of how Cohan tailored the recycled plot line to the particular talents of his own family.

The manuscript begins on page two with Susan Sweetapple and her friend Liz discussing how mischievous the errand boy Splinters is. There is an offstage crash and then Splinters enters, as if training for a prize fight. He jokes about not hitting another boy because he is smaller. Instead, he ambushed the boy's father with an ax handle. "He was over 87 years old. He ought to know how to scrap by this time."

(p. 4). Susan says she will tell the new master, who is arriving that day, to fire the errand boy. After she exits, Liz asks Splinter if he remembers the first time he saw her. He says he could never forget and the two do a song and dance.

After the exit of Liz and Splinters, the manuscript says "Intro: Man Who Broke the Bank" and Jolliett enters, probably to perform a song by that title. Susan enters and they talk.[8] Jolliett tells her that he has inherited his uncle's fortune because no will was found. He then asks for a drink. Susan replies "I hope you don't drink." He responds "Now I've enough money to stay drunk." He then asks why she wears the dress she has on. She tells him, "I belong to the Army, Sir," (p. 7) and Jolliett learns that his uncle used to be a member of the Salvation Army.

Jolliett informs Susan that he has invited a lady from New York to dine with him. Splinters then enters and is introduced to Jolliett.

Splinters: How de do. Shake.
Jolliett: The only thing I shake for is drink.

Jolliett: Splinters, there's a little dust on my coat.
Splinters: Yes Sir. (biz) *with broom* (Holds out hand) Haven't you forgotten something?
Jolliett: Yes, I've forgotten more than you ever knew. (pp. 9–10)[9]

Jolliett tells Susan that the lady he has invited to dinner is an actress.

Susan: Oh my, a horrible actress coming to this house.
Jolliett: That's it, a horrible actress. That's what she is. She's the worst actress I've ever seen. But talk about a dancer. Why she can kick nine feet over her head and can bend back and pick up a lobster with her eye. She's called the Human Cork Screw. I tell you Susan, she's a wonder. Why she's had her picture in the Police Gazette three times. (pp. 10–11.)

Susan then resigns. She tells Jolliett that she will marry Mr. McNulty, the town constable. Jolliett is surprised that she would marry "that bald headed, pudding faced old geyser McNulty." (p. 13.) Susan replies that she is leaving and will bring in her trunk to show that she is taking only what is hers.

Jolliett, who remembers being kicked by McNulty once, decides to hire a prize fighter to beat the constable. He rings for a servant and Splinters enters wearing boxing gloves. The errand boy brags about what a good fighter he is. Jolliett writes a nasty letter to the constable, which he does not sign, and gives it to Splinters to deliver.

After Splinters leaves, Susan enters with a calico dress that Jolliett's uncle had given her. She says, "I wanted to ask you if you didn't think it was awfully pretty.' (p. 16.) Just then the doorbell rings and she exits to answer it. Jolliett looks at the dress and says it's just like his uncle to give her such a cheap dress. He then says that it is unfair that Susan who worked for his uncle all her life got nothing while he got it all. Just then, the will falls out of the dress.

Jolliett picks up the will and begins to read it. "The last wool," he cracks. "[M]ust be connected with Mary's Little Lamb." (p. 17.) The will leaves the entire estate to Susan, except for $1.25 left for Jolliett.

Susan re-enters, explaining that the mailman was at the door with a letter for the cook. She then asks what is wrong with Jolliett, saying that he looks like a monkey in a menagerie. He replies, "Maybe I've gone back to first [illegible] a la Darwin. Susan, bring me a mirror. I want to see what I look like." (p. 18.)

While Susan gets the mirror, Jolliett decides to destroy the will. She brings the mirror and leaves. Jolliett wants a friend to confide in and decides to use himself in the mirror. If he placed Susan

> in possession of all this wealth, She'd die of joy and I'd be responsible for a murder. On the order [sic] hand, I'd die of dissapointment [sic]. Two murders. No. I'll destroy the paper. The will. I will. Ha. (Looks in mirror) Lord what a face. That's enough to frighten a politician into being honest. (p. 19–20.)

Jolliett then decides to show the will to Susan. He rings for her and tells her the will has been found in the calico dress. Susan is overjoyed and talks of how she will spend the money. In a sort of comic stychomythia, he alternates each of her joyful lines with a short lament. Susan finally decides to give the money to the Salvation Army. "That settles it," Jolliett replies, "I'll join the Army." She then asks what he will do. He answers, "I don't see any chance to do. It appears to me that I'm done." (p. 23.) Susan then offers him "ten dollars a month and all the work you can do," but only on the condition that he join the Salvation Army. She then gives him a Salvation Army cap. Jolliett reflects, "There's a record for you. A millionaire and a tramp all inside of an hour and a half. I never saw a young man go through a fortune so quickly in all my life." (p. 24.)

Susan goes off to find work for him to do, and there is a crash and pistol noise. Splinters enters in very soiled condition after his fight with the constable. Susan enters, gives irons to Jolliett to clean, and then tells Splinters that she is the new mistress. If he wants to work for her, he must join the Army. If he doesn't want the job, he can work the constable McNulty who, she knows, is looking for an errand boy. Splinters immediately decides to work for her and she gives him an Army cap. There is an indication for stage business with the cap. (p. 25–26.)

After the business, the doorbell rings and Splinters goes to answer it. Susan tells Jolliett to wash the dishes when he has finished the irons.

> Jolliett: Alright Susan.
> Susan: Susan?
> Jolliett: I mean Mistress.
> Susan: That's much better. (p. 27.)

Splinters returns to say that a young lady, Miss Carrie de Banner, has arrived to see Mr. Jolliett. Susan tells Splinters to have the young person step this way. Carrie enters, greets Jolliett and asks if he is actually working? "No, just exercising," he replies. (p. 28). Carrie tells him to order her some wine and asks if the others are his servants. He says they are and she introduces herself with a song, Gay Paree.

At the end of the song, Susan tells Carrie that the house is hers now. "I'll have no such actions as this within its walls." (p. 28) Jolliett then has to explain his situation to Carrie, who calls him a wretch and a monster. Susan says not to be too hard on Jolliett.

> Susan: His honesty brought him where he is.
> Carrie: I don't wish to talk to you at all. And as for you, you have grossly insulted me Sir. I shall have you arrested at once. (Starts to go)
> Jolliett: Where are you going?
> Carrie: I'm going to the law. If this town has a constable, I will bring him here. (Splinters hollers and exits. Carrie exits OP)[10]
> Jolliett: It isn't bad enough to give away a fortune and become a dishwasher. But now I've got to be humiliated by being arrested by McNulty.
> Susan: Poor Alphonso. Everyone seems so glad of his downfall that I almost wish the will hadn't been found at all.
> Jolliett: (aside) I wonder what my Mistress thinks of me now.
> Susan: Alphonso.
> Jolliett: Yes Miss. (pp. 29–30)

The manuscript ends at this point. The piece closed, according to one review, with a burlesque Salvation Army parade, which brought down the house.[11] After examining the other missing will stories, it is safe to assume that Susan destroyed the will and that she and the newly-reformed Jolliett were married.

"Money to Burn" is a good example of Cohan's vaudeville writing and contains elements which later became characteristic of his Broadway musicals. The script illustrates how Cohan wrote directly for production in both vaudeville and the legitimate theatre. His sketches (and later his Broadway plays) were blueprints for performance rather than literary compositions, and the performance of the Four Cohans, in a script tailored to their talents, made "Money to Burn" successful. Jerry and Helen Cohan, as Alphonso and Susan, had sentimental comic roles that reflected their own personalities and carried the narrative, while George, as Splinters, and Josie, as Liz and Carrie, excelled in their specialties. Yet the children received most of the attention in reviews of the sketch. Obviously, their personality and talent were more important than the story, and George's sketch highlighted those talents. Josie continually praised for her dancing, was now mentioned for her comedy work as well. The *Dramatic Mirror* described George as "one of the most promising young comedians on the stage," and found his character dancing "remarkable for its quaint originality."[12]

The sketch also provides an example of Cohan's use of contemporary events for his subject matter. In this sketch, George M. Cohan used the Salvation Army, with its recognizable uniforms and street-corner evangelism, as a target for comedy. Audience readily recognized both Susan's zeal and Jolliett's reluctance to join. Even the name Carrier De Banner is a pun about the Salvation Army.

After first performing "Money to Burn" in California in March, they premiered their new act at Tony Pastor's on September 13, 1897. The new sketch firmly cemented their position as vaudeville headliners, as a November 1897 article in the New York *Dramatic Mirror* suggests.[13]

Around the turn of the century, Cohan wanted to become successful on the Broadway stage and he began writing three-act musicals for Broadway. His first full length musical was an expanded version of his vaudeville sketch "The Governor's Son." After writing and producing two more musicals, Cohan produced *Forty-Five Minutes from Broadway* in 1905. (It opened in New York on January 1, 1906.)

Forty-Five Minutes from Broadway, the third production in the "missing will cycle," shows how Cohan expanded a short sketch into a full length musical play.[14] This 1906 musical hit starring Fay Templeton and Victor Moore, expanded the basic missing will plot to three acts and splits the leading male figure of the earlier versions into two separate characters: Tom Bennett, the rakish heir, played by Donald Brian, and Kid Burns, his "personal secretary," played by Victor

Moore. Bennett brings his fiance, the actress Flora Dora Dean, and her mother Mrs. Dean to his newly-inherited estate in New Rochelle, New York, only "Forty-Five Minutes from Broadway." The Kid, a wise-cracking, fast-talking, Broadway type, becomes the love interest of Mary Jane Jenkins, the housemaid, who contemplates the name that both their mothers had in common in the song "Mary." Mary has been jilted by Dan Cronin, a local businessman, when he discovers that she will not inherit the estate. Burns discovers that Mrs. Dean had some shady dealings with Cronin in the past. Burns then finds the missing will, naming Mary as heir, in a suit that was left to the butler. When he tries to tell his employer Mr. Bennett that his bride-to-be and prospective mother-in-law are up to no good, Bennett fires Burns. Before the play is over, the bride's mother helps Cronin try to rob the mansion safe, but is foiled by Mary. The next day, the house-maid, who had been continually insulted by Mrs. Dean, prepares to leave town (setting up the song "So Long Mary"), but she is stopped by Kid Burns, who shows her the will. After all the villains are caught, the two shyly express their affection for each other. When the Kid says he couldn't marry a woman with a million dollars, Mary tears up the will and the curtain falls.[15]

"Money to Burn," along with "A Noble Sacrifice" and *Forty-Five Minutes from Broadway* clearly illustrates how one simple plot device can be transformed by the differing needs of specific popular entertainment forms. From a two person act, to a four person musical vaudeville sketch to a full length musical comedy, Jerry J. and George M. Cohan's missing will plays used the same story to entertain their audiences. Unconcerned with an original story, Cohan took his father's plot device and using his own distinctive style turned it into two of his most successful productions: a vaudeville sketch that made his family headliners and one of his most popular and success-ful musical comedies.

ENDNOTES:

[1]George M. Cohan, handwritten manuscript of "Money to Burn," The Museum of the City of New York (no acc. no., in "Miscellaneous Sketches – GMC" box).

[2]Ashton Stevens's interview with Cohan, quoted in Ward Morehouse, *George M. Cohan: Prince of the American Theater* (New York: J. B. Lippincott Company, 1943), p. 57.

[3]New York *Clipper*, "Variety and Minstrelsy," November 28, 1896, p. 615; "Miner's Bowery Theatre," December 12, 1896, p. 652.

[4]New York *Clipper*, "Vaudeville and Minstrel," March 27, 1897, p. 56.

[5]Jerry J. Cohan, "Cohan Family Repertoire Book," MS Thr 226, Harvard The-

atre Collection. This notebook contains sketches, monologues and songs written by Jerry Cohan.

[6]"Vaudeville and Minstrel," New York *Clipper*, March 27, 1897, p. 56.

[7]"Tony Pastors," *New York Dramatic Mirror*, September 25, 1897, p. 18.

[8]The manuscript includes some stage directions. Susan enters "RH2E." That is, she enters from the second set of wings on the stage right side. (p.5)

[9]Cohan repeated the same joke in his 1906 musical *George Washington, Jr.* Cohan, *George Washington Jr.*, typescript, Act 2, pp. 1–2, Museum of the City of New York, acc. no. 68.123.330C.

[10]Opposite the prompt side of the stage.

[11]"Tony Pastor's," New York *Dramatic Mirror*, September 25, 1897, p. 18.

[12]"The Four Cohans," New York *Dramatic Mirror*, November 13, 1897, p. 18.

[13]"The Four Cohans."

[14]There are typescripts of *Forty-Five Minutes from Broadway* in both the Museum of the City of New York, and the Billy Rose Theatre Collection, The New York Public Library for the Performing Arts.

[15]Unfortunately for those who believe in happy endings, when Cohan wrote another show for Victor Moore as Kid Burns, *The Talk of New York* in 1907, Mary was not included in the cast. (Fay Templeton married industrialist William Patterson and retired from the stage in 1906. She also realized that Moore had the real starring role in *Forty-Five Minutes from Broadway*.) In the sequel, Kid Burns mentions Mary's name regretfully, as if he had lost her. His new love interest was played by Emma Littlefield, Victor Moore's wife. There was no mention of how Mary would fare, with no husband and no inheritance.

THE BOSTON GLOBE—TUESDAY. FEBRUARY 6, 1900.

CADETS' GLORIOUS STAGE PAGEANT.

Records of the Past Excelled by Boston's Crack Corps of Soldier-Actors in "Miladi and the Musketeer."

Illustration from *The Boston Globe*, February 6, 1900. From the microform collection, Boston Public Library.

Uncredited photograph montage from the souvenir program for *Simple Simon* (1897). Billy Rose Theatre Collection, The New York Public Library for the Performing Arts.

THE MEN OF THE DANCING FIRST

by Eugenia Everett

Popular entertainment in Boston at the turn-of-the-century was epitomized by the Massachusetts First Corps of Cadets. Despite the fact that they were an amateur group, their high standards of achievement made their productions the most anticipated event of Boston's winter theatre season.

The First Corps of Cadets, originally part of the Massachusetts Volunteer Militia, was formed in 1741 to function as bodyguards for the governor of the Massachusetts Bay Colony. The Corps remained active as a distinct unit throughout the nineteenth and during the early part of the twentieth century.

It was during the last decade of the nineteenth century that the Cadets made their mark on Boston's theatre community. In 1889 the men decided to stage a minstrel show to benefit the building of a new armory. The show ran February 13 and 14 (1889) at the Music Hall. It proved such a success that the Cadets decided to stage another show the following year. The 1890 show was a musical entitled *Injured Innocents* which ran for two nights, April 11 and 12, at the Boston Theatre. The reception of *Injured Innocents* was so overwhelmingly favorable that the play was presented again the next year for a six night run, January 12–17, 1891. That second production of *Injured Innocents* was given at the Tremont Street Theatre and marked the beginning of a decade-long association between the First corps of Cadets and the Tremont Street Theatre, which hosted all of the Cadets' productions until their final curtain in 1906.

Beginning in 1889, the Cadet musical was an almost annual event. Following is a list of the titles and dates of productions.

EUGENIA EVERETT holds a Master of Fine Arts in Dance History and Criticism from York University. She is currently working on a biography of Melvin Ballou Gilbert, a turn-of-the-century dance educator and choreographer.

Minstrel Show	1889
Injured Innocents	1890
Injured Innocents	1891
1492	1892
Tobasco	1894
Excelsior, Jr.	1895
Strange Adventures of	
Jack & the Beanstalk	1896
Simple Simon	1897
Queen of the Ballet	1898
Miladi & the Musketeer	1900
The Cap of Fortune	1902
Cinderella & the Prince	1904
Boodle & Co.	1905
Miss Pocahontas	1906

All the Cadet productions, with the exception of the first two, were given a full week's run – six evening performances and one Saturday matinee. The musicals proved to be phenomenal money makers and the Cadets spent a great deal of time during the year preparing for them. While there were many people who contributed to the productions over the years, only one man, Robert A. Barnet, was responsible for writing and directing all thirteen plays.

Barnet (1853–1933) was by trade a merchandise broker. Besides writing and directing, he performed in some of the early Cadet shows. He eventually left the Boston business world to write full-time for a theatre in New York City, but it was with the Cadets that he made his show business reputation. Barnet's plays were predictable for their thin plot lines which provided just enough of an excuse for the singing and dancing which composed the greater part of the plays. Each play contained dozens of female roles which were played by the men. *Miladi & the Musketeer* (1900) is a good example of a typical Cadet play.

Miladi & the Musketeer was a burlesque on the famous Dumas work. The musical was in three acts and the plot of the play hinged on finding twelve diamonds. In the first act Buckingham, the Queen, Richelieu, D'Artagnan and Miladi meet in the streets. The Queen, as memento of her love for Buckingham, gives him a pawn ticket representing the diamonds. The search for the diamonds is carried on in Calais during the second act; and in the third act the diamonds are finally found hidden in the ballroom of the Louvre. The principal characters were supported by a cast of over one hundred men representing the queen's armored guard, citizens of Calais, royal scrubwomen, Parisians and the king's own ballet company. The music was by George Lowell Tracy and the choreography by Melvin Ballou Gilbert.

The critics were unanimous in their praise for every part of the production. "It was one of those rare occasions where bright dialogue, tuneful music and graceful dances given by clever performers appealed to the best tastes of a refined audience."[1] The *Boston Globe* lauded the efforts of the chorus members saying, "The corps never before has shown anything as elaborate in the way of costuming, scenery and ballets, and although the principals naturally attract the greater attention individually, it is to the splendid contributions by the ballet and chorus that much of the success is due. In short, it is the ensemble work that deserves the larger share of praise for making the production a success of gigantic proportions."[2]

The members of the ballet had been rehearsing twice a week for four months before the play. Judging from the following comments in the (Boston) *Herald* their hard work payed off:

> The Cadets have always given fine exhibitions of their dexterous dancing powers, but last evening fairly outdid themselves. The most intricate and really the ballet triumph of all Cadet performances was given in the ballroom scene by 24 coryphees and the four 'royal dancers.' The dainty costumes of the dancers, the ingenious and charmingly picturesque groupings, the elaborate weaving of the figures, the profusion of the beautiful living tableaux, with their clever and brilliantly artistic manipulation of flower garlands and bouquets provided by far and most attractive and interesting ballet that had been seen here for many and many a day. Not only this, for the dancing of these femininely attired men was of a lightness and airy grace quite as exceptional.[3]

Men performing women's roles en travesti is certainly nothing new, but men performing seriously, as ballerinas, en pointe (in toe shoes) – amateur men at that – was a little extraordinary. Given what the corps de ballet in these plays were wearing, it is surprising they could walk, let alone dance. One of the Cadet principal dancers, Mr. M. W. Greene, described in a personal letter the process of dressing for a Cadet production.

> My waist was punished the most – corsets are the invention of the evil one! My waist measures naturally 32 inches, but gradually tightening of the corsets for several weeks I got so that I only measured 22 inches when dressed up. I could not breathe naturally of course, and after my solo dance each performance it seemed as if I should choke before I got my breath again. I was awfully afraid every time that I danced that my lacings and

clothing would burst. My practicing for several weeks gave me confidence in my motions, and as I stiffened my big toe joints inside the ballet slippers, I learned to dance on the tips of my toes, but oh–how it hurt me sometimes! The dressing and making up took two hours fully every time. I had to be shaved all over you know, face, neck, bosoms, arms, and hands. My legs were put into symetricals which made them shapely, and gave me the regulation female hips and rump. The liquid pearl that was freely put all over my face, arms and bosoms hardened on stiffly. Plumpers fitted over my face and an extension kept my nose from expanding and contracting when breathing. I had to have my own hair cut short and the wig of blonde hair which I wore was secured on by springs. The corsets laced on the two sides. It took over half an hour to lace me. I never ate anything until after I was laced, so as to have my stomach empty. The corsets were the stiffest made, and the shaping of the bosoms was done with piles of raw cotton which stuffed of the corsets from under my arms. The tights of black silk were drawn on after I got shaped. It had to be done for me–I could not do it myself. The ballet slippers were then put on for me–I could not now bend over. The voluminous black tulle skirt came next and was laced at the waist. The face, neck, and arms next came in for attention and then the wig. The long black kid gloves were tied up on my arms securely. The waist of my costume came last, it laced on at the back and was stiffened as much as it could be.

I could not see my feet nor could I see my waist, except in a glass, when dressed. A stiff black collar around my neck concealed the Adams apple and also covered up the cords of my neck. After a few minutes dance you can have no idea how I felt. If I pressed my hands to my heart, it was more to relieve the lungs than from any other cause. At the Thursday night performance I broke one of the side steels in my corset when doing the kicking act and the ends of broken steel nearly killed me before I could get them out.[4]

The men, like Mr. Greene, who took part in these plays were bankers, merchants, lawyers, brokers, accountants–white collar professional men. Most of the men appeared in several consecutive Cadet productions, thereby gaining some degree of proficiency in their acting, dancing and vocal skills. The critic from the Boston *Herald* noted in his review of the Cadets' last play *Miss Pocahontas* (1906), "A Cadet show is one that no longer excites wonder. It has come to be taken for granted that it will be a performance which in many respects will bear comparison with the work of professionals, and these almost annual productions have steadily grown in popularity until they have come to be assuredly one of the really important events of the social season."[5]

Cadet plays, by all critical accounts, were always well attended: and, as mentioned earlier, were the primary source funding the building of their new armory. One of their earliest plays, the week long run of *Injured Innocents* in 1891 netted them $10,000.00. Six years later, in 1897, *Simple Simon's*, net receipts totalled $25,000.00.[6] Each year the best seats were sold at an auction held approximately three weeks before the opening date. Any remaining seats were sold at the box office which usually opened a week or so after the auction. While the monies raised by the Cadets' productions were primarily used for their armory, the men occasionally donated both their time and money to help out in a community crisis. At the beginning of their run of *Queen of the Ballet* in 1898, a huge fire in downtown Boston claimed the lives of several firemen. The Cadets responded by adding an extra matinee performance for the benefit of the families of the deceased.

The imposing granite armory still stands today in Boston's Back Bay. In 1973 it was listed in the National Register of Historic Places and was designated a landmark by the Boston Landmark Commission in 1977. Across the top of one of the doors the words "First Corps of Cadets" sculpted out of the stone, identify the building's first occupants. Hidden in the cornerstone of the building is a time capsule which tells the story of the Cadets and how their armory came to be. Amongst other historical material that the Cadets placed in the capsule, can be found the souvenir programs from their first musical productions.

The Cadets had set out to build an armory. Their musicals helped them to realize that goal; and the quality of their productions made the Cadets the most popular entertainment troupe in Boston at the turn of the century.

Documents, souvenir programs, correspondence and scrapbooks pertaining to the First Corps of Cadets were found at the following libraries: the Boston Public Library, Boston University's Mugar Memorial Library, the Theatre Collection at Harvard University, and the Billy Rose Theatre Collection of The New York Public Library at Lincoln Center.

ENDNOTES

[1]"Great Hit: Cadets Surpass All Previous Records." *Boston Herald* 6 Feb. 1900: 4.

[2]"Cadets Glorious Stage Pageant." *Boston Globe* 6 Feb. 1900: 1.

³"Great Hit. . . .," *Boston Herald* 6 Feb. 1900: 7.

⁴ M. W. Greene, personal letter, part of the uncatalogued file on the Massachusetts First corps of Cadets at the Harvard University Theatre Collection.

⁵"Pocahontas Amid Big Skyscrapers," *Boston Herald* 6 Feb. 1906: 4.

⁶Melvin B. Gilbert, *The Director* (1898; New York: Dance Horizons, n.d.) 42.

⁷*Simple Simon*, souvenir program, Boston 1897: 24E.

SOURCES:

"At the Play." *Boston Sunday Journal* 2 Feb. 1902: 18.

"Audience Pays Extraordinary Compliment to Cadet Show." *Boston Globe* 14 March 1905, morning ed.: 4.

Barnet, Robert A. Clippings, Billy Rose Theatre Collection, The New York Public Library.

"Behind the Scenes with the Cadets." *Boston Sunday Journal* 9 Feb. 1902: 15.

Boodle & Co. Souvenir Program, Boston: 1905.

"The Cadet Show." *Boston Herald* 31 Jan. 1904: 17.

"Cadet Show Dancer Who Aims to be an Actor Like His Father." *Boston Herald* 6 Feb. 1902: 3.

"The Cadets and the Caricaturist of the Herald." *Boston Herald* 7 Feb. 1902: 9.

"Cadets Score Another Hit." *Boston Daily Advertiser* 4 Feb. 1902: 10.

"Cadets Score Another Triumph in 'The Cap of Fortune'." *Boston Globe* 4 Feb. 1902, morning ed.: 7.

Cap of Fortune. Souvenir Program, Boston: 1902.

" 'Cap of Fortune,' New Play of the Cadets Delights a Gay and Critical Audience." *Boston Herald* 4 Feb. 1902: 14.

Cinderella and the Prince. Souvenir Program, Boston: 1904.

" 'Cinderella and the Prince' Opens to a Houseful." *Boston Globe* 2 Feb. 1904, morning ed.: 7.

"Delightfully Catchy Music and Comic Absurdities Abound in 'Miss Pocahontas,' The Cadets New Show." *Boston Globe* 6 Feb. 1906, morning ed.: 5.

Everett, Eugenia. *Melvin Ballou Gilbert: Turn-of-the-Century American Dance Educator.* M.F.A. Thesis, York U, North York, Ont., 1983.

Excelsior Jr. Souvenir Program, Boston, 1895.

1492. Souvenir Program, Boston, 1892.

Injured Innocents. Souvenir Program, Boston, 1891.

Massachusetts First Corps of Cadets. Uncatalogued file at the Harvard Theatre Collection.

Miladi and the Musketeer. Souvenir Program, Boston, 1900.

Miss Pocahontas. Souvenir Program, Boston, 1906.

"Plays and Players." *Boston Sunday Herald* 2 Feb. 1902: 13.

"Pocahontas Amid Big Skyscrapers." *Boston Herald* 6 Feb. 1906: 1+.

"Prince's Graceful Dancing." *Boston Daily Advertiser* 1 Feb. 1902: 5.

Queen of the Ballet. Souvenir Program, Boston, 1898.

Simple Simon. Souvenir Program, Boston, 1897.

Strange Adventures of Jack & the Beanstalk. Souvenir Program, Boston, 1896.

"Three Cadet Players Who Are in Clover." *Boston Globe* 7 Feb. 1902, morning
    ed.: 7.
Tobasco. Souvenir Program, Boston, 1894.
"Triumph for Cadets." *Boston Herald* 2 Feb. 1904: 1+.